The Developing Child

The Developing Child

Using Jungian Type to Understand Children

Elizabeth Murphy

Davies-Black Publishing
Palo Alto, California

Published by Davies-Black Publishing, a division of CPP, Inc., 3803 E. Bayshore Road, Palo Alto, CA 94303; 800-624-1765.

Special discounts on bulk quantities of Davies-Black books are available to corporations, professional associations, and other organizations. For details, contact the Director of Book Marketing and Sales at Davies-Black Publishing; 650-691-9123; fax 650-623-9271.

Visit the Davies-Black Publishing Web site at www.daviesblack.com.

07 06 05 04 03   17 16 15 14 13 12

Printed in the United States of America

Library of Congress Cataloging-in-Publication Data
Murphy, Elizabeth
    The developing child : using Jungian type to understand children
 / Elizabeth Murphy.
        p.   cm.
    Includes bibilographical references.
    ISBN 0-89106-060-X
    1. Personality and children. 2. Individual differences in children.
    3. Myers-Briggs Type Indicator. 4. Children and adults. 5. Child rearing.
    I. Title.
    BF723.P4M87   1992
    1554'18264—dc20   92-29717
                                                                          CIP

FIRST EDITION
First printing 1992

*This book is dedicated to
all those who strive to build
positive adult-child relationships,
especially those in my home.*

Contents

Preface

Adults frequently reminisce about their childhood, remembering things that people said or did to them that inspired them or caused them pain. Stories about such episodes are often repeated to give a glimpse of how one person can influence another. People also remember significant phrases that others have used in conversations with them that spoke directly to their hearts or minds. Since comments by adults carry so much hidden power with children, it seems important to try to understand the ways that adults and children communicate and develop strategies for improving the bonds between them.

The concepts of psychological type provide a workable framework for understanding differences between children and adults that have an impact on the way they communicate with one another. The descriptions of the various type characteristics provided in this book can help adults and children better understand each other's behaviors and comments. By understanding each of the sixteen psychological types, adults can increase their awareness of more effective ways to help children grow and develop their special gifts and talents.

This book gives adults an opportunity to examine some suggested paths for developing positive relationships with the children in their lives. Examples are used to show how psychological type theory applies to daily life. The more that children and adults understand one another, the better their chances of building strong relationships. Each generation passes its knowledge onto another. This generation of adults can be the initial thread in the cloth that is woven to create enhanced relationships with children.

CHAPTER 1

■ ■

Jungian Type
and Child Development

Most parents expecting their first child believe that if they do everything right, their child will develop with minimal problems and family relationships will thrive. No one plans problems, although many families face problems as their children develop into adulthood. This book does not address the needs of children faced with special mental or physical challenges, but focuses instead on the relationships and learning needs of children following predictable developmental sequences. Most adults find that children are more enjoyable on some days than on others and despite all efforts, will find it difficult to tolerate some behaviors. How can adults begin to understand and differentiate the acceptable and unacceptable behavior of children? One way is by using the concepts of psychological type. According to theories based on the work of Carl Jung and Isabel Briggs Myers, there are sixteen psychological types, a combination of which begin developing in childhood and continue developing throughout lifetime. Psychological type provides a framework for understanding the way children's personalities develop and helps explain the different reactions of adults to specific behaviors. This book focuses on the ways in which the normal, natural personality differences of adults and children can affect the development of relationships between adults and children. These relationships include the family relationships between parents and children and the school relationships between teachers and students.

The material in this book about children and their relationships with adults is based primarily on experience. Not everything described has been proven or supported by research because the research is as yet incomplete. Some longitudinal research has begun, but more is needed to fully explain the richness of personality development in children. If the information contained in this book makes sense to you, then it serves a purpose *now* while researchers continue to investigate child development in their pursuit to find a definitive model to describe the emergence of personality in children.

All aspects of a child's development need to be considered.

To look at the developing child, the physical, intellectual, social, and personality development are all factors that need to be considered. Separate theories have been proposed for each of these factors. Theories about the physical development of children take the most predictable path. Average ranges for growth have been determined, and a child either falls within the average range for height, weight, and other factors, or a child exceeds or falls below the average range. Theories about intellectual development focus on cognitive skills that are acquired at particular life stages and provide numerical ranges that indicate a child's potential ability. Information on intelligence ranges do not predict how much a child will achieve or the ways a child prefers to learn. Social development focuses on children's acclimation to the world and to the people around them. Certain skills are required for living in society, and these are acquired as children develop. How children choose to respond to the world around them seems more closely related to personality development.

Personality is the one human component that provides the greatest insight into how children form their social relationships and how they prefer to learn. This book focuses on the normal personality differences between people. Instead of relying on one chart to identify normal ranges, multiple paths are used to explain normal personality development.

Type preferences don't predict behavior.

It is important for adults to recognize the role of psychological type preferences in relationships and behavior. Being aware of and having an understanding of type preferences will not enable adults to predict a child's behavior, but it can help them to understand the way a child *prefers* to learn and process information and the way a child *prefers* to communicate. That is, each individual develops a natural preference for taking in information and making decisions about that information. This preference is a choice of one of two possible alternatives, but the word *choice* is important here. For example, a child may like chocolate ice cream better than strawberry and most times, when given a choice, will choose chocolate. One day the child may decide to choose strawberry—to experience a change perhaps. Choosing strawberry doesn't change the fact that the child's usual preference is for chocolate, yet this doesn't prohibit the child from selecting strawberry whenever the time is right. An adult might make an educated guess that the child will choose chocolate but can't predict with certainty that this will happen because the child has free will. The same applies to differences in psychological types. A child may *prefer* to process information one way but has the free will to choose his or her preferred or nonpreferred path for any given situation.

Being aware of a child's preferences can help adults make better educated guesses about how children prefer to learn and communicate. It will not provide a simple formula that predicts behavior in all circumstances. Sometimes it is as important to know that a child is behaving in a way opposite a natural preference because this can be stressful for the child. An awareness of a child's preferences sensitizes adults and improves relationships. This book addresses the characteristics of the different psychological types as well as provides suggestions for how adults working with children can make use of these differences to improve communication.

Children with the same psychological type share common characteristics, but each child is an individual.

Some adults who first learn about psychological type become concerned that identifying the personality preferences of children is merely a way of putting a box around them and potentially limiting their full development. These same adults often fear that identifying personality preferences might predetermine how people will interact with one another. This would be a way of using knowledge of psychological type to restrict individual choice and it contradicts one of the primary messages of type development, which is to honor and encourage all individuals to develop the talents natural to their types and to learn the skills of people who have opposite preferences.

Jung clarified that human beings have commonalities with others who share their type preference but that each individual is also unique. Each person brings to the world a personality preference, but each is also exposed to a unique environment that shapes individual development and the expression of personality. The value of understanding type preferences and personality development is that it provides a usable framework to interpret the growth and development of individuals.

This book should help adults understand the template of normal personality development that begins in childhood and continues through adulthood. The descriptions of type in this book are examples and should not be interpreted as predictors of behavior. People should be understood for their uniqueness as well as for their commonality with others who share their preferences.

The personality preferences of adults are important.

Before adults attempt to understand children, they should make some effort to understand themselves in the context of psychological type. Adults are encouraged to review some of the available information about psychological type and to identify their natural preferences. Resources that may be helpful are listed at the back of this book. It is important that both parents and teachers know and understand how their personalities can influence the kinds of experiences that will be emphasized in the home or the classroom. This understanding also plays a role in helping to explain a child's behavior. Other books have adequately addressed the personality types of adults. The focus of this book examines the process of personality development in children and explores how an understanding of personality differences can improve relationships between adults and children.

Summary

Understanding the paths of a child's development provides information to enhance this development. An awareness of personality development is one aspect of the child's nature that adults can study to better understand the developing child.

- Psychological type describes the normal personality preferences of children and adults.

- Little longitudinal research involving children is available, so many of the examples used in this book are based on experience rather than on formal research.

- Personality development is only one facet of the developing child.

- Type preferences do *not* predict behavior.

- People with the same psychological type share a set of common characteristics, but each person is uniquely individual.

- The descriptions of type behaviors in this book are examples. Children who have the same preference will not necessarily conform to the descriptions or behave identically.

- Adults might consider studying the type preferences of adults as well as children. Recognizing the way different personality types interact can improve relationships.

CHAPTER 2

■ ■

Psychological Type and Type Development

Communication is easier when people use a common language. This chapter introduces the terms commonly used to describe psychological types and discusses personality development in greater detail. Each of the psychological types will be further described in later chapters. Some readers may prefer reviewing the terminology presented in this chapter first, then reading the chapters that discuss specific personality types and returning to this chapter later. If the information about type development in this chapter seems complicated, try reading the sections beginning with Chapter 3 that describe the different psychological types. Once you feel comfortable with your understanding of these differences, then return to this chapter to learn more about how these differences develop. Descriptions of type characteristics and type development work together and must both be understood, but which is studied first isn't important.

An introduction to the basic terms in this book

Extraversion/Introversion

People interact with their world in two ways—through an *extraverted* orientation or through an *introverted* one. Extraverts tend to be outer directed with their energies; introverts are typically inner directed. Chapter 3, "Interacting With the World: Extraversion and Introversion," explains how these differences can be recognized behaviorally in children.

Sensing/Intuition

There are two primary ways for people to perceive information. Those with a *sensing* preference tend to notice and focus on the information they perceive through their five senses. Those with an *intuitive* preference also take in information through the senses but quickly assimilate it into a pattern which becomes central to their focus. Ways to recognize these preferences in children are described in Chapter 4, "Taking In the World: Sensing and Intuition."

Thinking/Feeling

There are two possible ways for people to make decisions about the information they perceive. People with a *thinking* orientation tend to make decisions based on objectivity and logic. People with a *feeling* orientation are more likely to make decisions based on value systems. Ways to recognize these preferences in children are described in Chapter 5, "Making Decisions: Thinking and Feeling."

Judging/Perceiving

Individuals prefer a judging orientation or a perceiving orientation. Those with a judging preference value closure and like clear limits. Those with a perceiving preference value spontaneity and flexibility. This preference also indicates whether individuals prefer to use the sensing/intuition or thinking/feeling preference when they engage in extraverted activities. We cannot necessarily know what someone is thinking, but we can observe behaviors that help identify which preference the individual chooses. Since sensing and intuition explain how a person perceives information, this is considered the *perceiving pair* of preferences. Because people are thought to make judgments about the information they make decisions about, thinking and feeling, which focuses on decision making, is considered the *judging pair* of preferences. Certain behaviors are evident when people prefer to use their perceiving type (sensing/intuition) or their judging type (thinking/feeling). These behaviors are described in Chapter 6, "Observable Behaviors: Judging and Perceiving."

E/I   S/N   T/F   J/P

One strategy for introducing type concepts to children begins with the educator or other adult asking children to name a shorter way to say "television." Children quickly respond by saying TV. They are then asked which word they use more often—TV or television. Most say TV. When asked why, they usually say it's because TV is easier to say than the longer word television. Children find it easy to understand that people who talk about type use a similar shortcut when describing type characteristics: The first letter of the eight terms is used as the abbreviation for that word. E stands for extraversion, I stands for introversion, S for sensing, T for thinking, F for feeling, J for judging, and P for perceiving. Because introversion and intuition begin with the same letter, it cannot be used for both, so the second letter N is used for intuition. These letters combine in different ways to represent the sixteen psychological types.

Because each individual has a preference for one of the orientations in each of the four type pairs, a person's psychological type is represented by the letter that stands for that person's four preferences. A person prefers either extraversion or introversion, so the first letter in a type profile is either E or I. Likewise, a person prefers either sensing or intuition, so the second letter in a type profile will be S or N. A person also prefers either thinking or feeling, so the third letter will be T or F. Finally, a person prefers either judging or perceiving, so the fourth letter will be J or P. Choosing one preference from each of these pairs produces sixteen different possible types as shown in Figure 1.

Figure 1. Possible Type Combinations

ISTJ	ISFJ	INFJ	INTJ
ISTP	ISFP	INFP	INTP
ESTP	ESFP	ENFP	ENTP
ESTJ	ESFJ	ENFJ	ENTJ

A person's type is represented by the four-letter combination that stands for an individual's preference on each of the four paired scales. When asked, "What is your type?" a person familiar with type would typically respond by giving one of the sixteen four-letter combinations, such as INFP or ESTJ.

Children develop these preferences. During the course of development, however, a child may not have a clear preference. In these cases, the child's profile would use the letter U for Undetermined for that scale. For example, if a child preferred introversion (I), feeling (F), and perceiving (P) but did not have a clear preference for sensing or intuition, the four-letter combination would read IUFP. The letter U can represent an undetermined preference on any of the four scales.

Myers-Briggs Type Indicator® (MBTI®)

This personality inventory developed by Isabel Briggs Myers and Katharine Briggs identifies the sixteen psychological types. People who wish to take the instrument must have it administered by a trained professional such as a psychologist, counselor, some clergy members, or others who have met qualifying criteria. The MBTI has been used primarily with older adolescents and adults.

Murphy-Meisgeier Type Indicator for Children (MMTIC)

This instrument identifies the type preferences of children in grades two through twelve. It, too, must be administered by trained professionals and is often used to assist teachers in working with students and their individual learning styles.

Attitude

In psychological type, the term *attitude* describes the way a person chooses to interact with the world. The two scales that focus on this interaction are extraversion/introversion and judging/perceiving. The E/I and J/P scales are therefore referred to as the *attitudes*. Possible attitude combinations are EJ, EP, IJ, and IP.

Function

When people wonder about how something works, they are curious about how it functions. The sensing/intuition and thinking/feeling scales explain how individuals prefer to take in information and process it—or how they function internally with information. The S/N and T/F scales are therefore referred to as the *functions*. Possible function combinations are SF, ST, NF, and NT.

Preference

A preference indicates that one choice is favored over another. The less-preferred choice is acceptable—just not favored. Type describes psychological *preferences*. A person can use both sensing and intuition but will prefer one and will therefore find it easier to use. A common comparison is the way people use their right and left hands. For example, if a person is right-handed, he or she will write more smoothly and comfortably with it. If the person must write with the left hand, the penmanship is less legible and writing requires more effort. The same is true of psychological preferences. Use of a person's preferred style of taking in information (S/N) or making decisions about it (T/F) will seem easier and more natural. The less-preferred style can be used when necessary but will require more energy and effort and most likely will be executed with less skill.

The Unconscious

Part of the activities of the human personality can be found in the conscious; the remaining parts lie in the unconscious. People are aware of thoughts and feelings that begin in their consciousness but are less aware of those that occur in the unconscious. Thoughts and feelings constantly shift between the conscious and the unconscious, moving back and forth at a given moment.

Type develops throughout life.

An individual's personality develops throughout a lifetime. Jung stated that if children's personalities had the richness of adult personalities, they would be robbed of their childhood because childhood was the time for developing. When personality development is explained to children, a flower and seed analogy is often used. The comparison goes like this: A seed is planted and develops a stem first, then leaves, then a bud, then a blossom. The stem itself does not reveal what the blossom will be, and the blossom cannot grow until a stem and leaves have developed. If a sunflower seed is planted, the only plant that will grow is a sunflower. Similarly, as a child's personality develops, it can only develop into the innate preferred pattern of one of the sixteen possible type combinations. People can spend a lifetime using their less-preferred functions, but their innate preferences will remain unchanged. Adults sometimes make the observation that they were totally different as children but feel more comfortable with who they are as adults, often citing environmental influences to explain the differences. When given the freedom to be themselves, people's natural preferences emerge.

The functions develop as people age, but the attitudes are established early.

The attitudes—EJ, EP, IJ, and IP—seem to be stable from birth and do not seem to change as people age. For example, people who prefer to relate to the world in an extraverted way continue to prefer extraversion throughout their lives. People are simply more comfortable using their preferred attitude throughout their lifetimes. This preference for attitude becomes apparent from an early age and does not appear to fluctuate. Jung (Hull, 1971) emphasized that the attitude must come natural to the person and not result from environmental influences: "The fact that children often exhibit a typical attitude quite unmistakably even in their earliest years forces us to assume that it cannot be the struggle for existence in the ordinary sense that determines a particular attitude" (p. 332).

In contrast, the functions—SF, ST, NF, and NT—develop differently. These seem to develop over a person's lifetime. During childhood, the strongest preference develops. This could be any of the functions (S, N, T, F). Once developed, this function becomes the *dominant* part of a person's personality. During adolescence or early adulthood, the second preferred function develops. This is called the *auxiliary* part of a person's personality and must support the dominant function in every way possible. If the dominant preference is a perceiving function (S or N), then the auxiliary preference must be a judging function (T or F). Conversely, if the dominant preference is a judging function (T or F), then the auxiliary preference must provide balance and be a perceiving function (S or N). Developing a dominant and auxiliary preference means the child will develop a preference for one perceiving and for one judging function. The attitude preference for extraversion or introversion and for judging or perceiving remains constant.

By early adulthood, a third function develops, which is referred to as the *tertiary* function. If the dominant function is the strongest part of the personality, then its opposite function will develop last. The tertiary function is therefore the opposite of the auxiliary function, so if a person's auxiliary preference is sensing, then that person's tertiary preference will be intuition. If a person's auxiliary preference is intuition, then that person's tertiary preference will be sensing. If a person's auxiliary preference is thinking, then the tertiary function will be feeling, and if a person's auxiliary preference is feeling, then the tertiary preference will be thinking.

At some point in adulthood, the fourth function develops. This fourth function is called the *inferior* function and is the opposite of the person's dominant preference. The inferior function is so called because it is the last to develop. During the growing years, a person may not be able to use the inferior function as effectively or efficiently and may have a difficult time meeting task expectations that require the use of the inferior function. An awareness of a person's dominant, auxiliary, tertiary, and inferior function helps others understand how much an individual must stretch to meet certain task expectations.

If a person's dominant preference is thinking, the inferior function will be feeling. If the dominant preference is feeling, then the inferior function will be thinking. If the dominant is sensing, then the inferior function will be intuition, and if the dominant is intuition, then the inferior function will be sensing. Even though this inferior function does develop, its effectiveness as a part of the personality is less developed and less mature than all the other functions. A description of the dominant, auxiliary, tertiary, and inferior functions for each of the sixteen types is shown in Figure 2.

Figure 2. Functions for the Sixteen Types

ISTJ	ISFJ	INFJ	INTJ
Functions: ST	Functions: SF	Functions: NF	Functions: NT
Dominant: Sensing	Dominant: Sensing	Dominant: Intuition	Dominant: Intuition
Auxiliary: Thinking	Auxiliary: Feeling	Auxiliary: Feeling	Auxiliary: Thinking
Tertiary: Feeling	Tertiary: Thinking	Tertiary: Thinking	Tertiary: Feeling
Inferior: Intuition	Inferior: Intuition	Inferior: Sensing	Inferior: Sensing

ISTP	ISFP	INFP	INTP
Functions: ST	Functions: SF	Functions: NF	Functions: NT
Dominant: Thinking	Dominant: Feeling	Dominant: Feeling	Dominant: Thinking
Auxiliary: Sensing	Auxiliary: Sensing	Auxiliary: Intuition	Auxiliary: Intuition
Tertiary: Intuition	Tertiary: Intuition	Tertiary: Sensing	Tertiary: Sensing
Inferior: Feeling	Inferior: Thinking	Inferior: Thinking	Inferior: Feeling

ESTP	ESFP	ENFP	ENTP
Functions: ST	Functions: SF	Functions: NF	Functions: NT
Dominant: Sensing	Dominant: Sensing	Dominant: Intuition	Dominant: Intuition
Auxiliary: Thinking	Auxiliary: Feeling	Auxiliary: Feeling	Auxiliary: Thinking
Tertiary: Feeling	Tertiary: Thinking	Tertiary: Thinking	Tertiary: Feeling
Inferior: Intuition	Inferior: Intuition	Inferior: Sensing	Inferior: Sensing

ESTJ	ESFJ	ENFJ	ENTJ
Functions: ST	Functions: SF	Functions: NF	Functions: NT
Dominant: Thinking	Dominant: Feeling	Dominant: Feeling	Dominant: Thinking
Auxiliary: Sensing	Auxiliary: Sensing	Auxiliary: Intuition	Auxiliary: Intuition
Tertiary: Intuition	Tertiary: Intuition	Tertiary: Sensing	Tertiary: Sensing
Inferior: Feeling	Inferior: Thinking	Inferior: Thinking	Inferior: Feeling

People of the same type do not necessarily act alike.

There will be some similarities in the behavior of people who have the same type preferences, but people are not precise duplicates of one another. When presenting these ideas to children, it is helpful to use the sunflower analogy again, explaining that some seeds fall on rocks, while others fall in water, in good soil, or in not-so-good soil. Each seed will still become a sunflower, yet each of the plants is distinctive because of the way the environment influences its growth and development. In much the same way, individuals with the same type preference will share similar characteristics but will develop different personalities as a result of environmental influences. People's innate preference never changes, but the way they express that preference can be affected. Wickes (1966) underscores the danger of not allowing the natural preferences of children to be utilized as follows.

All functions exist in either their developed or undeveloped state. Without an opportunity to practice the use of a function, the child will be left with a function that remains undeveloped or underdeveloped. This lack of development affects how the child thinks and acts. One important concept is that no function disappears from lack of use. An undeveloped or underdeveloped function continues to affect behaviors in the conscious or unconscious nature of the child. Behaviors affected by an undeveloped or underdeveloped function will be less mature and less effective than behaviors affected by a well-developed function. Therefore, it is critical that children be given an opportunity to develop preferred functions. The information is this book is geared toward helping adults create conducive environments for encouraging children to develop their natural gifts by developing their preferred functions.

The process of personality development is sometimes referred to as *differentiation.*

The functions begin in the unconscious and through development become part of the conscious. Jung (Hull, 1971) described the development of differences as the "separation of parts from a whole" (p. 425). When the function becomes part of the conscious, it can then be directed. Jung felt that only the dominant function could truly be directed. The auxiliary, tertiary, and inferior functions never become totally part of the conscious because some parts remain in the unconscious. As a result, individuals tend to use their dominant function as the leading part of their personality.

Jung also felt that what he referred to as the *undifferentiated* function was characterized by ambivalence (Hull, 1971). This is apparent in the behavior of young children. It is easier to determine through behavior whether children prefer extraversion or introversion or judging or perceiving because these are attitudes. The functions are more difficult to determine—they are related to the reception and processing of information and these functions are not yet differentiated in children. A child will appear to prefer sensing one day and intuition the next, or feeling one day and thinking the next. Until the dominant function becomes differentiated, all the functions will appear immature and ambivalent. It is important that adults working with children understand that personality growth and development will occur only when children have had ample opportunities to explore all the functions until they naturally become more comfortable with one. Practice using the different functions will help differentiation to occur.

Functions cannot develop simultaneously.

People sometimes wonder if it would be better to develop all the functions simultaneously. Would it be better, for example, to develop the sensing, intuition, thinking, and feeling functions by letting each emerge a little at a time? Jung felt that the functions could not be developed simultaneously and that doing so would inhibit individuals from effective development. It is better for the dominant function to develop and lead the personality while a child is still developing socially. The effective use of one function is better than the ineffective use of all underdeveloped functions.

Imagine, for example, that you are a member of an audience listening to four speakers each presenting an important message. All four people are speaking at once. Most people find that they are able to listen a little to one speaker and a little to another. Most can't listen to all four at once and still understand the full message. Attempting to develop all four functions equally is a bit like trying to listen to four people talk at the same time. When one function is developed sufficiently to lead the personality, the individual has stronger direction.

An individual has a preference for either extraversion or introversion. This is easy to recognize in children because the functions are undifferentiated. As individuals develop, the process becomes more complex. No one is just introverted or just extraverted. In the case of each of the sixteen personality preferences, one function will be extraverted and the other will be introverted. If the dominant function is extraverted, then the auxiliary function will be introverted. If the dominant function is introverted, then the auxiliary function will be extraverted. In this way, personality is balanced. Each of the sixteen types has one perceiving function (S or N) and one judging function (T or F), and one of these functions is extraverted and the other is introverted. This preference of a perceiving and a judging function also provides balance to the developing personality.

The functions develop through practice.

How then does a function develop, and how does it become differentiated? Myers (1980) explains that individuals develop a function by repeatedly using it. Children must be given opportunities to use a function in their daily lives for the function to develop. This need to practice using a function applies to the development of the dominant and auxiliary functions. For example, assume the child established a preference for feeling as the dominant function. The child is comfortable and sure that feeling describes his or her dominant preference. Feeling is a judging function. Now that the judging function is identified, the personality tries to balance the developmental process by focusing on the perceiving functions (S/N). The child's energies begin to focus on sensing and intuition, and more attention is paid to how information is perceived. The child might try a sensing approach one day and an intuitive another, or the child may use sensing fairly strongly for a longer period of time—even up to a year before switching and devoting as much time to intuitive approaches.

More of the child's comments and actions focus attention on the perception of information. Because of this increased concentration of energy on these perceiving functions, an observer not as familiar with the child might assume that either sensing or intuition is now dominant because this function is the current focus of attention. It isn't that the child is changing a dominant preference but rather that the child is developing a preference for the auxiliary function. Repeated practice is necessary for the development of the auxiliary function just as it is for the dominant function. Because practice is needed to develop preferences, it isn't possible to determine a child's preference by observing a small sample of behaviors. An observer can infer the preference used for a particular situation but not infer that the child is using a preferred dominant or auxiliary function. An obvious expression of preferences over time yields the greatest insight into a child's true personality preferences.

For type to develop, children must have the freedom to express type preferences.

If the natural preference of a child is not valued or respected at home or at school, the child might be influenced to behave differently. This can occur, for example, with introverted parents who do not want their child to experience the stress associated with their memories of growing up introverted or with extraverted adults who simply don't understand the needs of an introvert. When adults encourage or reward extraverted behaviors in children who are introverted, they reinforce those behaviors and then begin to see the children demonstrate more extraverted behaviors. Such children do not actually change their natural preference for introversion. For example, extraverted parents might think it is important for their child to be involved in a lot of outside activities to get a wide range of experiences and to meet a variety of people. The parents sign the child up for soccer, softball, youth groups, dance, scouting, and music. Before each registration, the parent asks, "Do you want to sign up?" If the child wants to please the parent, the answer will be yes, even though all the after-school group activity is draining for the child. Their adapted behaviors merely present a false image. An introverted child will behave like an extravert if extraverted behaviors are what adults appear to value. The child's introverted characteristics will resurface at any point in the child's life when introverted behaviors seem acceptable. It is more frustrating for people to operate in their less-preferred functions and attitudes, so expecting an introverted child to act extraverted most of the time produces stress. The stress must be relieved in some way and may appear in the form of other symptoms.

Summary

An awareness of type terms and the developmental nature of type is a beginning step to learning about adult and child differences. Specific descriptions of each of the attitudes and functions are found in the next several chapters. A listing of the characteristics can be misleading unless there is also an understanding of how type develops in children. Characteristics can be studied prior to developmental issues, but an awareness of both type development and type characteristics is necessary to appropriately apply type concepts to improve adult-child relationships.

- Preferences do not restrict people from using their less-preferred functions or attitudes.
- Type develops over a person's lifetime.
- The E/I and J/P attitudes become evident at an early age and do not appear to change.
- The S/N and T/F functions seem to develop over a person's lifetime.
- The dominant function develops first, followed by the auxiliary function, the tertiary function, and the fourth, or inferior, function.
- A personality is balanced in every way. A perceiving and a judging function form the dominant and auxiliary

functions. One of these functions will be extraverted and the other will be introverted.

- People with the same type preferences may behave differently as a result of environmental influences.

- Differentiation is a process that occurs over a lifetime and explains how functions develop from the unconscious to the conscious state. Differentiation enables one function to become the dominant leader of the personality.

- The functions develop when people have opportunities to practice using them.

- An understanding of type characteristics *and* type development is necessary for effective applications with children and adults.

CHAPTER 3

■ ■

Interacting With the World: Extraversion and Introversion

The attitudes of extraversion and introversion are easily observed even in very young children. The extraverted child is drawn to interact with the world and may touch things first and think to ask for permission later. Extraverts want to experience activities and enjoy telling about these experiences. In school, these children understand information better if given frequent opportunities to discuss it. The extravert draws energy by actively interacting in the world.

Introverted children prefer to observe before interacting. "Let me watch first" seems to be a motto. These children may not share their ideas until they finish thinking them through. In school extraverts may raise their hands to discuss thoughts still forming, while introverts will wait to raise their hands until their ideas have shape. The introverted child draws energy from introspection.

A child's preference for extraversion or introversion affects everything about daily life. Some of the conflicts between parent and child or teacher and student can be attributed to differences on this attitude. The conflict centers on how the child interacts more than on the content of the child's thinking. People expecting an outgoing, gregarious child can be bothered by an introvert's tendency to withdraw from new and strange situations. People expecting a child to listen before speaking can be bothered by an extraverted child who interrupts others with questions and/or comments. Conflicts may develop when the child's natural preference differs from the expectations of the parent or teacher.

Figure 3 lists characteristics of extraverted and introverted children. Such descriptions can be misleading if taken out of context. The characteristics should be viewed as examples of possible behaviors that children with these preferences demonstrate, not as absolute criteria for the preferences. These descriptions provide a means for adults to become aware of the possible variations in the behaviors of extraverted and introverted children, but should not be used to suppress an individual's uniqueness. Examples for applications of type in the home are followed by examples for applications in the school setting. Sometimes the examples are generic and apply to both the home and school setting.

Figure 3. Type Characteristics of Extraversion and Introversion

Children Who Prefer Extraversion (E)	*Children Who Prefer Introversion (I)*
▪ Like variety and action ▪ Learn better if given opportunities to talk about the information they are learning ▪ Demonstrate energy and enthusiasm for activities ▪ Are stimulated by and respond well to activities in the environment ▪ May be easily distracted ▪ May act before they think ▪ Are usually friendly, talkative, and easy to get to know ▪ Become energized when they interact with others ▪ May say things before thinking them through ▪ Have a shorter "wait time" between questions and answers than introverts	▪ Enjoy individual or small group activities ▪ Are energized by ideas ▪ Think before they act ▪ Carefully form ideas before talking about them ▪ Usually wait for others to make the first move ▪ Like to observe things before trying them ▪ May not share their thoughts and feelings with others ▪ Need time for privacy ▪ Dislike interruptions ▪ Pause before answering questions and have a longer "wait time" between questions and answers than extraverts ▪ Can ignore distractions ▪ May seem reserved and quiet

Extraverts and introverts express thoughts at different times.

Home Applications

Extraverted children are more likely than introverted children to share information at home. Some may even seem to be nonstop talkers. As extraverted children grow older, some of their expressed thoughts will not always be welcome. Children in junior high school often say things that are not their final thoughts. Parents who overreact to the undeveloped thoughts of some extraverted teenagers might inadvertently force these adolescents to defend viewpoints that never were final opinions. Oftentimes, because they tend to speak before they think, extraverts in hindsight say they wish they could put their words back into their mouths. If an extraverted child makes a comment, parents might want to determine if it is a final thought before they react to it. An adult might say to an extraverted child, "Do you really mean this? Is this your final idea?" If the answer is yes, the adult can then react. If it's not, then the adult can avoid reacting prematurely.

Parents can often recognize the energy of extraverted children but sometimes don't know what can be done with it. Telling an extraverted child to "sit quietly" or to "calm down" when something exciting is about to happen is much like attempting to stop a speeding train with a hand signal. It is against an extravert's nature to sit back quietly and wait for something to happen. A better approach would be to encourage the extravert to talk about the pending event as a way of expressing the excitement in an acceptable way.

School Applications

A strategy to ask extraverted children if what they said was what they meant to say was introduced during a training workshop with teachers. The school bell rang and the teachers returned to their classes for approximately fifteen minutes before they rejoined the training session. During that time, a middle-school student responded to a request to go the administration office by saying, "Make me." The teacher, remembering that extraverts sometimes blurt out comments before they think about them, said, "Is that what you really wanted to say?" The student answered, "No. I have no idea what made me say that." The student and teacher were able to resolve a small incident that could have escalated into a major issue if the child's comment were taken to mean more than it did.

Extraverted children have a great need to share their ideas. Young extraverted children often blurt out answers in class before the teacher calls on them to speak. The teacher often needs to remind these children to "please wait your turn." When the teacher does finally return to the extravert to give the child an opportunity to share again, the child has usually forgotten the idea that was so important to them a moment earlier. Some adults might believe that children who have important ideas would be able to remember them because, when they were children, they would have been able to remember their ideas. But the memory of extraverted children is constantly disrupted by an abundance of new thoughts and stimulations. Just because a child forgets an idea doesn't necessarily mean that the thought wasn't important. It only means that younger extraverted children need to be taught how to retain their thoughts until they have a chance to share them. In a later chapter we will explore ways for adults to build positive relationships with introverted and extraverted children.

Children cope with distractions differently based on their type.

Home Applications

Parents often wonder if children should be allowed to watch television while doing their homework. Extraverted and introverted children respond differently to distractions, so setting one rule for all family members may not necessarily amount to fair and equal treatment. Experience suggests that introverts dislike being interrupted and prefer to work in settings where there are limited distractions. Extraverts, in contrast, like to be distracted. Also worth noting is the fact that while introverts are initially annoyed by distractions, they are capable of blocking them out and concentrating when needed. Some introverted children whose preference also is for feeling and who just want to work in the company of others will do their homework in front of the TV. Because introverts can block out distractions, these children can complete their homework while the TV or radio is playing. Extraverts are drawn to distractions and have a difficult time blocking them out and concentrating. When extraverts must concentrate, a quiet setting provides a better study environment.

Based on this discussion, some parents might conclude that extraverts should not be allowed to do homework with a TV or radio on but that introverts should be allowed to. In reality, this at least depends in part on the kind of homework assignment the child is doing. Many homework assignments consist of review sheets or worksheets that do not necessarily require children to concentrate and think. If an extraverted child is doing an assignment that requires concentration, then the child will need a quiet setting. If the assignment only requires partial concentration, then the task can probably be done in front of the television.

Parents might set a rule that if a child is unable to complete the homework correctly after working in front of the TV for an hour, then the child must leave the room and work somewhere where there are no distractions. When extraverts really need to concentrate, they will likely search for a quiet place to work and complain that family members are making too much noise. Since frequently it is the extravert who is the noisemaker, their complaints may not be well received by family members. Because a child needed quiet one night does not mean that quiet will be needed every night. The difficulty of the assigned task will determine the amount of concentration that will be required.

This pull to notice all that is happening is important to respect in an extraverted child. Important information or important family discussions shouldn't be shared where many distractions are possible. Walking with the child through an amusement park is the wrong time for a parent to talk about issues they want the child to think about before reacting.

School Applications

Extraverted children in school love the opportunity to observe, watch, and interact. They want to be in the center of all that is happening. Sitting near a door or a window can be distracting for this child. The only time this is critical is when the child must *concentrate*. Two extraverted students can be taking the same test. For one the test is easy. Area distractions are not a critical issue. For the other extraverted child the test is quite difficult and every extraneous movement breaks the needed focus. Telling an extravert to "focus" or "concentrate" will not help. Both students described were extraverts but both students did not need to concentrate.

Introverts and extraverts respond differently to interactions.

Home Applications

Introverted children frequently want to be left alone for a while when they come home from school. Parents who don't understand this sometimes force children to interact with others. Some parents are so eager to hear about their child's day that they will ask countless questions in their attempts to draw the child to share. The introvert may be drained from interacting all day and may need some time to relax alone before being with others. Without understanding why, some introverts tend to answer probing questions with simple, to-the-point answers such as "No," "I don't know," or "Nothing." Some parents can become quite disturbed and may mislabel this behavior as avoidance or withdrawal and imagine that the child is having problems communicating. Some introverted children will talk endlessly once they are given an hour or so of privacy to regroup.

Sometimes introverted children don't respond to questions immediately or will retain their ideas until it can be proven to them that another idea is better. These children have been called stubborn. Introverts must reconcile new information with old ideas before accepting the change. This process does not occur spontaneously. Because introverts do their thinking internally, adults are unaware of an introvert's thinking. All the teacher or parent is aware of is silence. The silence can easily be misinterpreted as stubbornness, willfulness, or a lack of comprehension. The silence might actually provide the introvert with the time needed to internalize the new information.

Extraverted children can come home talking a thousand words a minute to anyone who will listen to them. Sometimes there is no real point to the discussion—the child just shares ideas. At the end of a day sitting in school, an extraverted child might prefer doing something. The worst rule for this child would be to do homework before being allowed to play.

School Applications

Teachers who expect extraverts to come in, sit down, and quietly begin to work are asking these children to act counter to their nature. Extraverts need some time first to say hello and engage with others in the class. Allowing children to have some interaction time prior to doing isolated assignments respects this extraverted need to interact with others.

Introverts among close friends will appear behaviorally to act extraverted. Among close friends, the introvert will enjoy interacting as much as the extravert. The difference seems to be that the introvert *enjoys* the opportunity for interaction with friends and the extravert *needs* an opportunity for these interactions.

Extraverts share. When ideas are flowing , words come out, and, since the ideas are still forming, the sequence of thoughts may not be precise. An extravert does not appreciate being interrupted with questions when ideas are flowing. Questions force the extravert to stop processing thoughts to focus on the question being asked. This can be irritating. A better strategy would be to wait until the extravert pauses before asking clarifying questions.

Introverts and extraverts share differently in group discussions.

Home and School Applications

If children are asked to join a group, introverts are less likely to take on the role of leader and direct the activities. This is especially true if the directions or the assignment is unclear. Extraverts are more willing to risk initiating activities and exploring as they work. In some group settings, extraverts can keep the pace of conversation flowing so rapidly that introverts do not feel comfortable making the necessary interruptions that would enable them to join the conversation. Introverts need a bit of silence to act as a door opener. Because extraverts sometimes feel uncomfortable with breaks in conversation, in a group setting they might interject more questions or more opinions as a way of stimulating the conversation. Unfortunately, this only keeps introverts silent and stagnates the conversation further. If one extravert is talking and another extravert begins to talk, the first speaker may feel stimulated to continue because the other person seems as interested in the topic as he or she is. If an introvert is talking and an extravert enthusiastically begins to share ideas also, the introvert may stop talking. The message the introvert receives is that the ideas are not valued so the introvert stops sharing. Some extraverts are amazed to discover that what they thought would stimulate conversation actually impedes it in the case of introverts.

The wait time for extraverts and introverts differs dramatically. Some extraverts assume that if a person is not saying anything, then it means that the person has nothing to say. Introverted silence can sometimes be perceived as agreement or as noninvolvement. Often introverts are unable to share their ideas because they haven't been formed yet. Introverts sometimes think back for hours and days about what they could have said or should have said in a past situation. A Nancy comic strip captured this tendency of introverts well. It pictured Nancy stating, "I'd probably win more arguments if there was a little less lag time to my snappy comebacks."

The style and pace of sharing ideas can conflict with teacher expectations.

School Applications

Extraverted children sometimes find that their learning style is not always valued by their teachers. Extraverts learn better if they are given opportunities to discuss the information while they are learning it. The process of talking through the information facilitates their ability to recall and process it. If extraverts are expected to sit in classrooms and listen to one teacher after another lecturing, they usually find other outlets for sharing their ideas by talking to friends.

One extraverted child in the first grade was moved to the back of the classroom as punishment for talking with his friends. The next day he got in trouble for yelling across the room. Defending his behavior, he explained that he had to yell "because the teacher moved me way in the back, and the only way my friends can hear me now is if I talk louder." He didn't seem to remember that he was moved to the back of the classroom in the first place because he talked. His need to talk with his friends was strong enough to overcome whatever obstacle distance presented. Some children have been taught to use a few hand signals or sign language so they can communicate with their friends without disturbing the teacher. It isn't the need to communicate that disturbs many teachers, but the noise that is generated when talking is the mode chosen for meeting this need. Sign language and secret signals can help solve this problem.

Teachers who are trying to generate an exciting energy-filled discussion can be irritated by the introvert's reluctance to share. Some teachers may think this reluctance stems from a problem with shyness and may try to encourage the child with comments such as, "Don't be shy," "Say what you think," or "We're all friends here. We just want to know your ideas." Introverted children don't hesitate to share just because of shyness. Many more hesitate because their ideas aren't clearly formed. By the time a teacher finishes with all the "encouraging" remarks, an introvert can think of something to say even if it isn't a final thought. Because the introvert gave some response, the teacher might continue to believe the initial hesitation was shyness instead of a hesitation because ideas weren't clearly formed.

Extraverted teachers find it draining to lead a discussion with an introverted group, and introverted teachers find it a challenge to control the focus of a discussion when some extraverted groups begin interacting. An understanding of the impact of extraversion and introversion on group interactions can help ease tense moments. A strategy to help extraverts and introverts is to give each child an index card. One side of the card can be green and the other can be red. (Marking pens can be used to make these cards.) When a group is discussing a topic, a child uses the green side to indicate that he or she has something to share and the red side to indicate that ideas are still forming. Red should not be taken to mean that the child has nothing to say but rather that the thought is in development. The teacher can call on green cards first. This strategy also eliminates the need for hand waving among children in the younger grades.

Summary

The introverted and extraverted attitudes describe important differences in the ways people interact. An appreciation of these differences can improve the living environment.

- The behaviors common to a particular type will not be evident in every child who is that type.
- Extraverts share their ideas while they are still forming them. Introverts wait until their thoughts are formed before they share them.
- Success for doing homework with distractions is determined by the child's type and the difficulty of the task.
- Extraverts are energized by interactions with others while introverts are drained by them.
- Extraverts who talk at the same time may stimulate additional comments. Extraverts who talk while introverts are talking often will stifle conversation.

CHAPTER 4

■ ■

Taking In the World: Sensing and Intuition

Sensing and intuition are the perceiving functions that describe how individuals prefer to process information. Sensing children take in information through the five senses. They pay attention to details and build conclusions based on the sequential organization of this information. Intuitives also take in information through the five senses but focus greater energies on reorganizing the information into patterns. The intuitive takes a holistic and global perspective, while the sensor examines the details and specifics. Sensors focus on the present while intuitives look toward the future. Descriptive examples of how these differences influence parent-child and teacher-child interactions are listed in Figure 4. These descriptions are only examples and should not be used to suppress individuality.

Sensing and intuitive children work at different rates.

Home and School Applications

Sensing children tend to work at a steady pace until they complete their work. If children are given a project to complete in six weeks, sensing children may pace their work and do a little each night, especially if they also prefer a judging attitude. Intuitive children may work a little one night, not work at all for two nights, work intensely the next night, not work on the project the next night, and so on. These bursts of productive energy are followed by lapses in energy that produce little or no work.

Figure 4. Type Characteristics of Sensing and Intuition

Children Who Prefer Sensing (S)	Children Who Prefer Intuition (N)
▪ Like precise directions ▪ Prefer using skills they've already learned ▪ Focus on the present ▪ Work at a steady pace ▪ Prefer step-by-step learning ▪ Rely on experience for learning rather than on what they read ▪ Are likely to have a good recall for details ▪ Draw on proven methods to solve current problems ▪ Want facts and examples to describe issues and mistrust vague ideas ▪ Focus on what actually is	▪ Need opportunities to be original ▪ Like tasks that require imagination ▪ Enjoy learning new skills more than mastering familiar ones ▪ Dislike routines ▪ Work in bursts of energy with slower, less productive periods in between ▪ Focus on the future ▪ May skip over facts or get them wrong ▪ Spend so much time on the design stage of a project that when finished often falls short of expectations ▪ Need variety ▪ Have a seemingly sporadic, random approach to learning ▪ Like to imagine what could be

Both types take in information through the five senses, but they process it differently.

Home and School Applications

Sometimes it is difficult to distinguish sensing children from intuitive children because the results of their work can look the same. Both types can reach the same conclusion but go about reaching the conclusion differently. A brother and sister had an older sibling who attended college and lived away from home. One day after school, the intuitive came home and said, "When did sis get home?" The mother asked, "How did you know she was home?" and the intuitive said, "I don't know, but she is, isn't she?" The sensing sibling would have reached the same conclusion but processed the information sequentially to reach an end. The sensor would have walked in the room, noticed the sister's sweater on the chair, smelled her familiar perfume, then turned to the mother and said, "When did sis get home?" The sensing child notices detail and then uses these details to reach a conclusion. The intuitive child takes in the information through the five senses but doesn't necessarily focus on the information itself. Instead, the intuitive forms a conclusion about the information perceived through the senses and may not recall specific details as much as form global impressions of the data that were taken in through the senses.

Creative processes are different for sensing and intuitive children.

School Applications

Sensing children and intuitive children are both creative, but approach the process of creativity from different perspectives. Sensing children work from the specific to the general, starting with their experience and looking for ways to modify what already exists—beginning with the parts and building up to a theme. Intuitive children work from the general to the specific, beginning with the theme, then trying to think of the parts needed to complete the theme. An example from an art lesson may help clarify this point.

The class was given a piece of drawing paper and told to make a picture. An intuitive child sat and thought, "What can I make? I know. I'll draw a picture of the sea. Now, what should I put in the sea? I think I'll put some fish, and a treasure chest, and some seaweed, and then a shark and a boat on top of the water." The sensing child started by drawing a fish. The fish looked good so the child added seaweed. Then the child added the treasure chest, the shark, and then the boat. Both children drew a picture of the sea, but the intuitive child began with the theme and later added details, while the sensing child began with the details that later evolved into a theme.

Sensing and intuitive children need different kinds of help completing work.

School Applications

Intuitive children seem to need help translating their designs into products, while sensing children seem to need help formulating the design. Once the project is designed, they are able to develop it.

Young intuitive children are able to mentally construct elaborate designs but are frequently unable to implement them in such a way that they equal their mental images. Their gift lies in being able to design, but they have not yet developed the necessary skills that will enable them to translate their design into a real thing. Intuitive children will need help learning how to find and use the materials that will help them meet the intricacy level of their image. Intuitive children who look at projects that don't meet their original intentions have commented, "I wish the teacher could see what I imagined. She would have really liked that."

Sensing children sometimes have a difficult time designing their projects. Again, an example of an art assignment may help to clarify this point. Students were given vague directions for completing a major art project. They weren't given any models or clear directions. The students could select any topic and use whichever medium they chose, but the finished product would constitute a major part of their semester grade. The sensing students had a difficult time knowing where to begin. Because the task was so broad, they needed help narrowing the topic.

Once the topic was defined more precisely, the students had a better sense of where to begin the task. In contrast, intuitive students working on this project needed help selecting and locating materials and assembling the project.

Childhood intuitive hunches are not equal to
adult intuitive hunches, and childhood sensing
experiences are not equal to adult sensing experiences.

Home and School Applications

Intuitive children differ from intuitive adults in that many do
not have as much faith in their "wild ideas" as adult intuitives. As
adults, many intuitives try to convince sensing adults that their
ideas will work because they have confidence in their ideas,
designs, and conclusions even before the details have been determined. As children, some intuitives will look around and wonder,
"How come I'm the only one with these ideas? Are these weird?
Are these any good?" Intuitive children feel somewhat insecure
about the quality of their intuitive leaping. Because clear preferences are established as children practice using each of the
functions, children will be less confident in their early attempts to
use the functions. Children may develop some consternation until
practice confirms that their intuitive "guesses" were good. The
intuitive conclusions gain credibility through repeated success.

Sensors use experience as a base for forming conclusions.
The first time an event is experienced, the sensor gathers information and carefully collects each sequence of the event that leads to
a reasonable conclusion. Once a mental path from data collection
to conclusion is experienced, a memory chain is established.
When similar situations occur, the sensor relies on this memory
of the experience to help reach conclusions more quickly. Adult
sensors have said, "I don't need to think about things very long
if I've done something like that before." The first time a child
works with fractions might take many examples and repeated
practice but once the concept is clear, the teacher can introduce
mixed fractions or improper fractions more easily because the
child has experience with fractions. The more experiences a
sensor has, the more likely it is that a path from the specific to the
general theme will be established. The more this path is established, the less there is a need for direct experience. Because of
their age, sensing children have not had as many opportunities for

experiences to form these memory chains. This means that new learning may be more difficult for the sensor until the sensing child builds an experiential path from the specific to the general. Because of their limited range of previous experiences, the needs of the sensing child for direct experience that builds on a sequential series of steps may be greater and more obvious in sensing children than in sensing adults.

Sensing and intuitive children need different information to get started on assignments.

Home Applications

Intuitive children need to know the main idea behind things and don't want to be bothered with a lot of details that seem unnecessary. One intuitive child was frustrated when her sensing parent helped her with her math homework. She only wanted to know one aspect of the problem, but her parent felt she should know and understand all the parts leading up to that step in order to fully understand the step. What happened was that the child stopped listening as the parent went through all the extra steps and began listening again once the parent explained the part related to her original question. The other information the parent provided was "extra" and the student had too much to do to be bothered with extra information at the time.

The reading styles of sensing and intuitive children differ.

Home and School Applications

Children differ in the way they read directions, skim through a text, and search for details. Sometimes the sensing child's natural style is an advantage and sometimes the intuitive child's style is preferred. Teachers who understand these differences are in a better position to help individual learners.

Children with an intuitive preference tend to skip reading directions. Many admit that they look at the examples provided for an assignment and figure out what to do on their own. Intuitive children also tend to skip passages in stories that focus on descriptive details or else scan them. The intuitive looks for the main idea in the story, and unless descriptive passages appear relevant to that goal, the details are passed over. When questioned later about the details in a story, the intuitive has a more difficult time recalling them.

Sensing children, in contrast, read everything in a story. They tend to begin with the first paragraph and continue reading until the end. Because they do not skim, they generally take longer to read the same information. When intuitive children finish reading sooner than sensing children, the sensing children assume it is because they are slow or stupid. If a teacher asks the intuitive child, "Did you read the chapter?" the child will honestly answer, "Yes." When the teacher probes further to find out if particular sections were thoroughly read, he or she will in all likelihood discover that the intuitive child skipped paragraphs because he or she had the general idea. Even though passages may have been skipped, the intuitive child believes the chapter was read. A sensing child is more likely to read every word.

Sensing children also tend to read directions, while intuitive children tend to assume that they know what to do. Intuitives are more apt to look for examples as a way to form their conclusion about the content of the directions. Sensing children value examples as a clarification of the directions, while intuitives value examples as a substitute for directions. Teachers can find comfort in the fact that multiple examples help clarify directions for all types.

Teachers will often begin a discussion by talking about the overall concepts of a chapter or telling students to finish reading the chapter for homework. Sensing children can be at a disadvantage in such instances if they haven't finished reading the chapter because they build their general idea of the concepts from all of the parts. Such children may therefore not form global impressions until they've read the entire chapter.

It sometimes helps to ask sensing children to formulate a single topic sentence to describe the section they just read before continuing to read the chapter. If allowed to write in the text, the children can be encouraged to write this topic or summary sentence in the margin. Then if children need to refer back to the text for answers to questions after they've read the work, they can use the summary sentences as clues for where to look first. Sensing children seem to need practice forming global statements. Intuitive children seem to need practice reading for details. When children are told what they should focus on prior to reading, the task becomes easier for them.

Students with sensing and intuitive preferences give directions differently. One student explained that her intuitive friend tried to teach her how to water ski. The friend told her to "grab the rope, bend your knees, hold on, and let the boat pull you up." Her sensing need was strong, and she countered her friend's directions by asking, "*How* do you grasp the rope, *how* do you bend your knees, *how* do you hold on, and *how* do you let the boat pull you up?" The lack of detail in her friend's directions made it difficult for the sensing friend to learn the task.

The need for details is different for sensing and intuitive children.

Home and School Applications

Sometimes sensing children have a difficult time understanding a concept because they have an intuitive teacher introduce the material at school and then have an intuitive parent attempt to help them study the concept at home. Adults working with sensing children need to respect the sensing child's need to gather as many pieces of information in a sequential way as are necessary to understand the concept. Sensing children may ask many questions while an intuitive adult is trying to explain something. These questions can be viewed as interruptions or delay tactics. They actually enable sensing children to gather information in a sequential order, which is necessary for them to understand. When sensing children feel there are gaps in the information presented, their response is to ask more questions.

Adults often assume that sensing children do not understand their explanations, and some sensing children will say they feel "dumb" because they have to ask so many questions. In reality, the intuitive adult has a tendency to offer few details. The total picture of a concept is clear in the mind of the intuitive, but since the details are considered weak, few are offered. Yet because the sensing child forms the image of a concept with details, the child must get them. When a piece of information is missing from an explanation, intuitive children will skip over the gap and assume that it will be filled in later. Sensing children will stop and attempt to get the information at that instant. If the bridge from one piece of information to the next is not built, sensing children do not feel comfortable taking the necessary leap and forming what appears to them to be unsubstantiated conclusions. The problem does not lie with the sensing child nor does it lie with the intuitive adult. The problem lies in the communication pattern that takes place between the two.

Sometimes when sensing children ask questions, intuitive adults respond by repeating the same information in a slower, more precise tone. It is as if the adult perceived that the children asked the questions because they could not comprehend the message. To the intuitive adult, the problem was with the receiver. Actually, the problem is with the sender of the message, too. Intuitives typically do not incorporate sufficient details when they explain some things to a sensor. When pressed for details, intuitives may be at a loss because they tend to overlook the details themselves. They may therefore respond to the request by repeating the global conclusions more carefully and slowly as a way of providing clarification. In the case of sensing children, a richer repertoire of details would provide better clarification.

Now let's reverse the combination. The adult prefers sensing and the child, intuition. A different communication problem develops. The sensing adult can inadvertently teach the young intuitive to doubt an intuitive leap at a time when the *intuitive* doubts these leaps. For example, a sensing teacher introduces a lesson on the history of a famous poet. The teacher asks, "How did he learn his craft when there were no schools?" An intuitive child begins brainstorming various possibilities. If the teacher says, "Where are your facts? How can you support your ideas?"

the subtle message is that the idea isn't good until it has supporting evidence. This message sends the child out of the intuitive mode and into a sensing mode to gather supporting details. The problem is that most intuitives gather information to support an intuitive idea. Gathering information without an end as a guide means they have no filter to know which information is relevant and which is not. This creates confusion. Without meaning to, the sensing teacher sends the message for the child to abandon intuition and use sensing skills. An intuitive child who already doubts intuitive leaping will develop more doubts about forming conclusions too soon. All students should learn to gather support for their position, but *first* the teacher needs to affirm the value of the intuitive leap. Instead of implying that a concept isn't valuable until it is supported, the teacher could say, "That's certainly possible. Are there other possibilities?" This statement acknowledges the worth of the intuitive leap. Then the teacher can ask, "Can anyone find information or details that could prove to someone that yours is the best possible conclusion?" These steps affirm the intuition first, then require the supporting details. The original remark by the teacher only stated the expectation for supporting details. Again, an understanding of the sensing and intuitive styles of processing information can become a tool to facilitate the learning of all children.

Both intuitive and sensing children like variety.

Home and School Applications

Intuitives are typically credited with enjoying variety. Actually, there is a subtle distinction that helps describe how both types value variety. Intuitives seem to enjoy simultaneous variety. These children like to be involved in many different projects at one time and are willing to abandon one project to begin a new project that appears more interesting to them. Sensing children also value variety but seem to favor sequential variety. Once sensing children have mastered a skill, they are ready and eager to look for something new to try. Until mastery is reached, sensing children seem to prefer focusing all their energy toward practicing and learning that particular skill. Sensors do enjoy repeating previously learned skills but for a limited time. They tend to look for variety once they master a skill.

The sensing preference for experience is not the same as the need for experience during the concrete stage of cognitive development.

School Applications

Some may confuse the characteristics of children who use a sensing preference with children who are in the Piagetian concrete operational stage of cognitive development. This is the stage of cognitive development most common during the elementary school years.

Children in the concrete stage of thinking rely on experience to learn information. The sensing child *values* concrete experiences, but this is a critical difference between the two. Children in the concrete operational stage of development are *experientially bound*, meaning they can only form abstract hypotheses about items in their experiential repertoire. Individuals with a sensing preference do not depend so exclusively on their experiences to learn and can be better termed as *experientially based*, using their sensing skills to gather information and then form abstract thoughts. Experiencing something in a concrete way does not limit them from using abstract reasoning to process the information.

Predicting the ending can be a game for some intuitive children.

Home and School Applications

Some intuitive children pride themselves in their skill of "guessing" what their friends are going to say. They use their intuitive leaps to determine what will come next, and then finish sentences for sensing children. This can be upsetting for the sensing child. Adults often will finish a sentence for a child, though perhaps they do it in a more gentle way. It is as if the intuitive wants to get to the point so they rush ahead without giving the other person a chance to complete the thought. Adult intuitives should try to appreciate that the sensing child's point may be to share the rich details about their day. There may be no other global conclusion than that. If one sibling does this to another, the parent might say to the intuitive sibling, "It's fun to try to figure out what someone is going to say so that you can later find out if you were right, but finishing someone else's idea for them can limit the person from sharing even more wonderful details. Please keep your guesses to yourself and try to listen to the details of the story."

Intuitive and sensing children have different reading habits.

Home and School Applications

Many intuitive children, particularly introverted intuitive children, enjoy reading books. They enjoy reading complete stories, so when the class has a contest to see who has read the most books, the intuitive has an edge over other students. Sensing students tend to read bits and pieces of information. When sensing students read, they read every word. When given a choice of *what* to read, the sensor tends to choose material that provides pieces of information. Many prefer reading magazines as opposed to novels. Long novels can be overwhelming for some sensing students, but they can conquer the long novel if they read it one chapter at a time. Many sensing students read lots of facts in newspapers or in books that assemble large quantities of information. They seem to enjoy books that cite lists of things like the "Ten Best..." or the "Ten Most Wanted...." A favorite selection of sensing children seems to be *The Guiness Book of World Records*. These children gather information. They enjoy reading small bits of information at a time. Magazines can provide a favorite source of information for these children. One problem sensing children encounter in school is that they have a difficult time writing book reports on this type of reading material. Adults working with children can learn to appreciate that there are many ways to encourage children to read. Reading the newspaper with the sensing child or listening to the intuitive child tell about the plot of a novel encourages each to use the strengths of his or her preferences.

Intuitive children are most attracted to possibilities, while sensing children are most invested in the here and now.

Jung (Hull, 1971) points out that intuitives may find it difficult to remain on tasks that seem to limit possibilities; it is important to them that variations seem to be possible. It will take more effort for an intuitive to concentrate on understanding what is than it will for the intuitive to imagine what might be.

Because intuitives are attracted by new and different projects, some may find it difficult to sustain attention to a task long enough to complete it. They may drift from one project to another because of their need for variety. Because their ideas change rapidly, the end project can develop into a product quite different than the original design. These students need help remaining focused on a task to completion. Sensing students who focus on the present may have difficulty projecting how the future will require changes in their original design.

Summary

Sensing and intuitive differences reflect the primary ways children perceive information. Because these functions are developing, accommodating a child's preferred style increases the chances for effective communication.

- Sensing children work at a steady pace, while intuitive children work in bursts of productivity followed by periods of unproductivity.

- Both sensing and intuitive children take in information through the five senses but process it differently.

- Both types are creative, but the sensing child begins working with the details and builds to a theme, while the intuitive child begins with a theme and adds details later.

- Intuitive children need help actualizing their designs, while sensing children need help planning their designs.

- Sensing children need to know the details, and intuitive children need to know the overall concept before they begin working.

- Sensing children read everything that is written, and intuitives skim what is written.

- Sensing children need details before they can build ideas. Intuitives often dismiss an abundance of details because these restrict them from considering more possibilities.

- Sensing children seem to enjoy sequential variety, while intuitive children seem to enjoy simultaneous variety.

- People who value experiences are not bound by their experiences or limited from making abstract conclusions. Children who are still in the concrete operational stage of cognitive development are bound by their experiences.

- Intuitive children prefer to read books, while sensing children prefer shorter works, such as magazines, short stories, and newspapers.

CHAPTER 5

■ ■

Making Decisions:
Thinking and Feeling

Thinking and feeling are the functions that describe how children make decisions. This function likely develops after sensing and intuition. Those with a thinking preference are able to make detached, objective decisions based on the information presented. These students value competence in themselves and others. They need to understand why rules exist. Thinkers use logic to prove their point. Those with a feeling preference make decisions based on value systems. These children value harmony and enjoy pleasing others. Those with a thinking preference try to prove they are right, while those with a feeling preference try to persuade others of their convictions. Examples of thinking and feeling behaviors in children describe how this function appears in the child's world and are shown in Figure 5.

Children of both types need affirmation.

School Applications

Many children with a feeling preference have difficulty working for teachers who do not like them. The first few weeks of school can be stressful for these children until they receive some reassurance that they are welcome. An example that occurred in one classroom during the first weeks of school may help demonstrate this point. A student with a feeling preference was working

Figure 5. Type Characteristics of Thinking and Feeling

Children Who Prefer Thinking (T)	Children Who Prefer Feeling (F)
• Value individual achievement more than group cooperation • Need to know why things are done • May find ideas or things more interesting than people • Need opportunities to demonstrate competence • Are concerned with truth and justice based on principles • Spontaneously analyze the flaws in ideas, things, or people • Need to know the criteria for grades and evaluations • Try to prove their points logically • In younger grades may enjoy talking with teachers more than with peers • May have difficulty accepting nonspecific praise	• Need feedback and praise about their performance • Avoid confrontation and conflict • Are skilled at understanding other people • Spontaneously appreciate the good in people • View things from a personal perspective • Are concerned about relationships and harmony • Enjoy pleasing people, even in seemingly unimportant matters • Enjoy subjects that concern people and need to know how decisions affect people • Have difficulty accepting criticism and can find sarcasm and ridicule devastating

at her desk when the teacher casually walked past her and said, "Your handwriting is sloppy." The student was upset and went home and said, "Do you know what the teacher said to me today? She said my handwriting is sloppy." Her mother responded, "But your handwriting *is* sloppy." The child answered, "But she said it."

For several weeks this student practiced her handwriting to impress the teacher. When she mentioned this to the teacher, the teacher said, "What?" The original comment about the handwriting being sloppy was just a casual observation to the teacher, yet the student took it to heart because a bond had not yet been formed and the issue over the handwriting was a potential threat to that bond. Near the time that the handwriting incident occurred, the teacher happened to write "You're a good student. I'm glad you're in my class" on one of the student's essays. That feedback was all that the student needed to feel valued. After that, the teacher could make constructive criticism that the student could accept. Once teachers establish a relationship with students and let feeling children know they are welcome in the class, they can accept corrective feedback. Feeling children appreciate receiving frequent reassurances throughout the school year.

A child with a thinking orientation might react quite differently to the teacher's comment about sloppy handwriting. At the time the comment was made, the student with a thinking preference might ask, "Will my handwriting affect my grade in this course?" If yes, how much?" The thinking student would be able to detach the person from the criticism to realize that the term "sloppy" applied only to handwriting and not to the total person. It would be important for the thinking student to know how handwriting skills affected the evaluation of classroom performance. Thinking children need affirmation that they will be evaluated fairly. They need a clear understanding of task expectations. It would be unfair for a teacher to deduct points for sloppy handwriting without telling the class that clear penmanship was expected.

Praise must be specific and credible to be accepted.

Home and School Applications

Children with a thinking preference seem able to determine when they have done something well, whereas children with a feeling preference rely on others to tell them so. Feedback is extremely important to feeling children because no feedback is equal in their minds to negative feedback. If the child has done something special at home to help or has done a special project for school, the adult needs to express his or her appreciation or the child will feel slighted. Parents who say, "They know I love them" or teachers who say, "They know I'm proud of them and I don't need to say it all the time," don't understand the needs of the feeling child. A general rule is that you can't tell feeling children too often that you enjoy their company and that you appreciate their effort and work.

Children with a thinking preference also value praise; however, these children want feedback about their competence. Praise must be specific to be credible. Statements such as "You're super!" have little meaning to these children unless you can explain why. Some adults are put off because an extraverted thinking child might ask, "Why did you say that?" or "Why am I super?" Adults who respond by saying, "You just are," have not really complimented a thinking child.

Children with thinking and feeling preferences express opinions differently.

Home and School Applications

Children with thinking preferences tend to say what they think. One parent reported that she was mortified to hear her daughter, who came in second place in a competition, talk with the winner. When the winner came over to speak to her daughter, the winner said, "I'm sorry you didn't win." Her daughter answered, "Why? That doesn't make sense, because if I won you would have lost." The parent felt the situation called for a more subtle, diplomatic response and wondered why her daughter acted so ungraciously. But the thinking child was not being ungracious; she was being direct and could not understand why her mother was upset with her.

Many people with a feeling preference find it difficult to say things directly so they soften the message, especially if it is negative, by using a lot of words or by using very gentle words. A child with a thinking preference might say, "That's weird." A child with a feeling preference might say, "That's different from things I'm used to." Both carry the same meaning, but one is direct and the other is indirect.

A daughter with a thinking preference was accused of saying mean things to her friends, but then her sister put her direct way of speaking in a more positive light by saying, "I know I can come to you and you'll tell it to me straight." Those with a thinking preference tend to analyze the situation based on current information and arrive at a conclusion. The sociability of the response isn't the issue; the truthfulness of the statement is.

Children with both preferences want rules to be fair.

Home and School Applications

Children with a thinking orientation have a difficult time when they think things are unfair. They expect rules to be fair and to be enforced the same for everyone. When adults impose rules on one child and not on another, it is difficult for the thinking child to accept. Feeling children do not seem to mind bending the rules if the situation warrants. An example from a monopoly game might help demonstrate this point. One player had gone around the game board and was out of money so he could not pay the rent due on a property with houses. The child with a feeling preference did not want to lose the friend from the game and said, "Never mind. Pay me sometime later." Another player with a thinking preference was irate that the rules were being altered. In her mind, everyone paid rent or no one paid rent, but the rules couldn't change each time. Both children had legitimate reasons for deciding to enforce or ignore the game rules. The thing to remember is that those with a thinking preference make their decisions objectively and those with a feeling preference make their decisions subjectively.

Thinking and feeling children don't always hear what others mean to say.

Home Applications

A woman had two children. One had a thinking preference and the other had a feeling preference. She took both children shopping with her to select some new clothes. After trying on the first dress, she came out of the fitting room and the thinking child said, "Boo—no." The feeling child said, "That's nice, but why don't you try on this one?" When the mother tried on the second outfit, the thinking child said, "That's so-so." The feeling child said, "That's nice, too, but try this skirt and sweater." By the time the mother tried on the third outfit, the thinking child was angry and said, "I'm not going to tell you what I think. Everything I say is the opposite of what she says. Who are you going to listen to, because you can't listen to both of us!" Actually, both children had agreed on how the outfits looked. The thinking child said it directly, and the feeling child softened her rejection of the outfits. The important point is that the thinking child was unaware of the similarity of their comments. He heard the beginning of her phrase, and because it sounded different he stopped listening to the "but..." part of her sentence. Communication conflicts often result because thinking children have a difficult time sifting through the abundance of words that feeling children may use to express their thoughts. The feeling child has a difficult time accepting the directness of the thinking child's opinion.

Children with a thinking preference need to know why.

Home and School Applications

This need to know the why behind things means that children with a thinking preference often ask why they have to do something or why something has to be. They have a real need to know the cause and effect and the reasoning behind decisions. Some adults perceive this inquisitiveness as a challenge to their authority. Their response to a child who asks why is often to say, "Because I said so and you don't need any more reason than that." The reality is that the adult reacted as if the authority were being challenged, when the child reacted out of a natural need to know the *why* in order to better understand the world. Adult comments such as "Because I said so" won't prevent children from asking why; they will only stop them from asking why out loud. It is inconsiderate to tell children with a thinking preference that they should do something "just because" and that they should not question each request. Thinking children must ask, must know, and must understand why if they are to comply with the requests made of them.

Children with a feeling preference may not ask why when they should. Sometimes these children are so eager to please that they follow requests so the other person won't get angry or be unhappy.

Children with a thinking preference are able to evaluate their skills, while children with a feeling preference depend on the opinion of others.

Home and School Applications

Children with a thinking preference seem more competent than feeling children at developing an independent image of their self-worth. They seem to recognize when they do well and when they don't. Feeling children do not seem to have this same sense of detachment that would allow them to evaluate their self-worth. Their evaluation depends on those around them. If the person they are with values them, then they feel they are valued. If the person they are with does not value them, then they do not feel valued. Many feeling children seem trapped by the evaluations of others. Children with a thinking preference have been known to say things like, "Well, they just don't know I'm the best." These thinking children have been accused of bragging when they think they are just stating the truth.

Children with a feeling preference need to develop some skills that will enable them to evaluate their worth without depending on the views of others. Feeling children, like many feeling adults, say that if ten people told them they did a good job and one person told them they didn't, they would believe the one and worry about what could be done to fix it so that everyone liked their work. On her syndicated talk show, Oprah Winfrey said that she was once so dependent on the opinion of others that if one person wrote to her and said they didn't like her shoes or her lipstick, she would contact the individual to discuss it. This need for resolving potential conflicts resembles the behavior of the feeling individual. The feeling individual is very sensitive to criticism from others. Feeling children must know they are liked, so even during the difficult preadolescent and adolescent years, feeling children need reassurance of their worth. Because the adolescent attempts to establish an independence from adults, this need for reassurance can get lost in the struggle for separation.

Children with a thinking preference need to permit themselves to make mistakes while learning a skill. Many of these children become frustrated during the learning phase of any skill because they expect themselves to do well. When their performance doesn't match this expectation, many work diligently to develop the skill until the gap is bridged. Working diligently is admirable, but until the gap is bridged the child is plagued by feelings of incompetence. The skill the thinking child needs to develop is a realistic pacing that enables the child to learn new tasks without experiencing frustration.

The preference for thinking or feeling can have an impact on what information children remember.

Home and School Applications

Sometimes an individual's preference influences the information they process. For example, two children, one with a feeling and one with a thinking preference, were reading a story about a bombing raid in London during World War II. As the class discussed the story, the child with a thinking preference reported that he couldn't even finish reading the story because he thought it was so stupid. The planes were going to bomb the city and the plane's lights were lit. If the story was going to be that stupid, it wasn't worth reading. No pilot going to bomb a city would make the plane a better shooting target by putting the plane's lights on. The child with a feeling preference totally overlooked that detail because she was so concerned that a bomb would hit the home of the protagonist's family. Her feeling function caused her to focus on the people in the story, while the child with the thinking preference had his concentration interrupted by the illogical use of tools in the story line. Type differences can help people understand why two students reading the same material will review it differently.

All children experience emotions, but these affect the decision-making process differently.

Because the term feeling is used to describe the rational thinking process, there is always some confusion about the distinction between the feeling function and actual feelings or emotions. People of *all personality types have feelings.* People with both feeling and thinking preferences have feelings. For some, it helps to separate emotions from the feeling function by categorizing emotions as affect or physical reactions and the feeling function as a form of rational judgment.

Jung (Hull, 1971) explains that using the feeling function to make a subjective decision would create no physical changes in the body. Experiencing feelings as an emotion means there is a physical response that accompanies the decision.

The physical changes to the body reflect affect or emotions. The process of using the feeling or thinking functions may be accompanied by affect. Although those with a thinking preference feel emotions, these emotions do not interfere with their ability to make independent, objective decisions.

For example, assume a child's parents recently divorced. The father lives away from home and invites the feeling child to visit that weekend because he's been feeling lonely. The child makes a decision to visit Dad. The decision is made with the feeling function but there are no physical responses, no emotions involved. Before she is told of the invitation, the mother asks the child to spend the weekend with her because she'd like some company. Now the feeling child has knots in the stomach because whichever choice is made, one parent will be left alone. The knot in the stomach is the physical emotion that accompanies the subjective, feeling decision-making process. The emotions interfere with the ability to decide, and it is difficult for the feeling child to abandon emotions to make a decision.

Jung felt the child with a thinking preference would experience empathy with each parent, perhaps would experience the knot in the stomach, but would put this emotion aside when making the decision where to spend the weekend. The thinking child might reason that the dad can call a friend if he is lonely or the mom can call a friend if she wants some company. The core question for the child remains: Now it is more important to spend time with _____. The feelings of empathy, the knot in the stomach, can be put aside in order to reason and make a decision. The feeling child cannot put aside the emotion.

People with a feeling preference make decisions based on value systems. The path that leads them from one piece of information to the next is not direct or linear. It can instead be circular. Logic is not a necessary tool that feeling types use to process information. Consider two elementary-aged children who were talking, one with a thinking preference and the other with a feeling preference. The feeling child said to the other, "Don't you believe me?" and the thinking child answered in a pleasant tone, "Of course, I just need you to prove it to me." Sometimes when children are asked to prove their point they feel that they are being questioned. Feeling children often have a difficult time separating themselves from the task at hand, their accomplishments, or their comments. Those with a thinking preference try to prove their point, while those with a feeling preference try to persuade.

Telling children with a feeling preference to get tough or to quit worrying ignores their natural sensitivities.

The self-esteem of each type develops differently.

Some people think that everyone develops a self-image similarly. Others believe that a positive self-image helps people cope with failures or short-term difficulties. Another possible interpretation about the development of self-esteem is that the self-esteem of people with a thinking preference develops differently than it does for people with a feeling preference. In this interpretation, events in the lives of those with thinking preferences can be likened to dirt on a mountain. Every good thing that happens to thinking types is like a cup of dirt put on the mountain, and every bad thing that happens to them is like a cup of dirt taken off of the mountain. As long as there are more good events than bad events, there is a balance, and the thinking individual is comfortable with his or her self-image. For those with a feeling preference, a comparison can be made to air in a balloon. Every good thing that happens in the lives of those with a feeling preference is like a puff of air into a balloon. The occurrence of one bad thing, such as someone harshly criticizing the feeling type, may cause the balloon to burst. In such instances, some people may try to help encourage feeling individuals by asking them to look at all the good things in their lives or asking them to evaluate whether the criticism was fair. Those with a feeling preference seem more comfortable if they can acknowledge the affect that accompanies their preference. Once feeling individuals take ownership of the physical affect that accompanies their bursting balloon, the better able they are to reach out to the problem and think rationally about it. The best approach is to let feeling children experience the unhappiness of the moment, because feeling children must focus on the affect of their unhappiness before they can think rationally. No matter how good the self-image of the feeling individual is, their balloon will pop.

Adults with a thinking preference who see children with a feeling preference looking devastated will often take their gift of logic and problem-solving skills and try to help. The feeling child, who is at that point immersed in miserable affect, doesn't necessarily need logic or help solving the problem. At the moment of the unhappiness, the feeling child only needs to be held, reassured, hugged, or consoled. Introverted feelers may not even want to discuss the issue that led to their deflated self-esteem. Extraverted feelers may discuss the event but may not want to problem solve or generate solutions. Once the depth of the affect has passed, the individual with a feeling preference will then be able to use the feeling function to rationally examine the issue.

The thinker has a difficult time seeing the feeling person's pain, so thinkers offer their natural gifts of logic and rational problem solving to try to help. Unfortunately, the message that feeling people receive is that they need to stop being the way they are, to change, to think logically and problem solve. If this is the message that the feeling person receives and it is not accompanied by any hugging or comforting, a wedge can be placed between the thinker and feeler. The feeling person will eventually not turn to the thinker for support during difficult times. This can be particularly critical in relationships between adults and children. It can be especially devastating when the difference occurs between parents and children who do not live together because of divorce or other family circumstances. Living apart from a child limits the adult's opportunities to be available for the child and, as a result, miscommunication that occurs in times of trouble takes on greater meaning.

Sometimes those with a thinking preference are placed in a compromising position. If, for example, you are a parent with a thinking preference and your feeling daughter, who is dressed to go out, comes to you and asks, "How do I look?", it is not a time to provide direct feedback that is negative. To tell her that she looks okay except for her hair leaves her susceptible to feeling miserable all night. In this example, there is little likelihood that there will be time for the child to change anything, since she is already dressed and ready to go out. The critical feedback would be better saved for another time. However, if the child asks you for your opinion about her appearance while she is fixing her hair, you can honestly say yes or no, because there is still time for a change to be made. Provide critical feedback to a feeling person when they can do something about a situation. If the situation can't be changed, the feedback may not be helpful to them.

Summary

Characteristics of thinking and feeling describe differences in the way children reach decisions. Relationship styles and relationship needs differ.

- Feeling children need to know they are welcome and appreciated. Those with a thinking preference need credible praise.

- Thinkers and feelers express the same thoughts differently.

- For thinking types, rules need to be fair. For feeling types, rules should help people.

- Those with a thinking preference have a need to know why.

- The self-esteem of thinkers and feelers forms differently.

- All types have emotions and affect. This is not the same thing as using the feeling function to make decisions.

■ ■

CHAPTER 6

Observable Behaviors: Judging and Perceiving

Judging and perceiving refers to a child's attitude. This attitude seems to exist from a young age. Those with a judging preference value time to prepare. They enjoy being prepared for a task and take pride in work completed. These children seem to appreciate clear guidelines and expectations from adults. Working against deadlines can be stressful for judging children. Those with a perceiving preference like to keep choices open and may delay making decisions. Rules are restrictive to them and can easily be forgotten. Deadlines provide the stimulus for effective thinking to emerge. The perceiving child enjoys change and spontaneity in the world. Examples of judging and perceiving differences help clarify how differences on this attitude interfere with positive adult-child interactions and are listed in Figure 6. An understanding of these differences helps in developing strategies for coping with, adapting to, and enhancing these differences in children.

Children with a judging preference seem to have "external order" and children with a perceiving preference seem to have "internal order."

Home and School Applications

Students with a judging preference have what some people refer to as *external order*. Their school materials are usually filed and arranged in their notebooks in an orderly manner. Their

Figure 6. Type Characteristics of Judging and Perceiving

Children Who Prefer Judging (J)	*Children Who Prefer Perceiving (P)*
<ul><li>Prefer expectations for tasks to be defined clearly</li><li>Like to get things settled and to get work done</li><li>Prefer completing one project before beginning another and can become stressed by too many unfinished projects</li><li>Don't usually appreciate surprises</li><li>Need predictability and can find frequent changes upsetting</li><li>Like to make decisions</li><li>Want to do things the "right" way and try to make things happen the way they're "supposed to"</li><li>Work best when assignments can be planned and the plan can be followed</li><li>Work well if tasks are paced and become frustrated with incomplete assignments when deadlines loom near</li><li>Do not like to mix work and play but would rather work hard first then play later</li><li>Seem to have a good sense of time and can predict how long it will take to complete tasks</li><li>Value the finished product rather than the process of doing something</li></ul>	<ul><li>Act spontaneously</li><li>Like freedom to move and become bored with too much desk work</li><li>Are cheerful and bring fun and laughter to the world</li><li>Enjoy the process of doing something more than the finished product</li><li>Work and play simultaneously and try to make work fun</li><li>Enjoy the unplanned and the unexpected</li><li>Adapt well to change</li><li>May start too many projects at once and have difficulty finishing them</li><li>Let work accumulate and then accomplish a lot with a last-minute flurry of activity</li><li>May turn in assignments late as a result of poor planning or time management</li><li>Work better against a deadline</li></ul>

desks are usually clear of extraneous pieces of paper. Their external world is orderly. In contrast, students with a perceiving preference are sometimes said to have *internal order*. Their desks may look chaotic, but they can usually locate materials upon request. This ability to find things in what may appear to be chaos is a skill that develops with the perceiving child, so it is not uncommon for younger perceiving children to be less adept at locating missing items.

Rules are important to judging children and perceiving children in different ways.

School Applications

Young children are often accused of being tattletales when they tell teachers that someone is breaking a rule. When this happens between siblings, there is a greater likelihood that the child is tattling on the sibling to get him or her into trouble. But in some of the younger elementary grades, there is another possible explanation. Children with a judging preference must know what the rules are so they can be good and follow them. When another child breaks the rules, the judging child will often tell the teacher. For example, a teacher has a rule that the children are not to play beyond the yellow line on the playground. A child runs to the teacher and says, "Johnny crossed the yellow line. Is he in trouble?" Teachers usually say they don't listen to tattletales and will often ask the tattling child to leave. For many judging children, what the question really meant was, "Johnny crossed the yellow line. Are we allowed to cross the line now? If we are, I want to cross it, too, but if we aren't, I don't want to break the rule. So which is it?" In other words, the punishment of Johnny confirms for the judging student that the rule still stands.

Perceiving children seem to have more difficulty remembering rules. They may violate rules simply because they live so spontaneously that they act before they have time to think about the rules. There is also an indifference to rules. Rules exist for other children and if they can be ignored, they will be. Perceiving children may test rules to be sure they are going to be enforced. Teachers who enforce a rule one day and not the next will suggest to the perceiving student that the rule can be broken. Many perceiving children see rules as barriers rather than guidelines. When working with perceiving children, a good guideline is to have as few rules as possible.

Children with a judging preference work first, then play; children with a perceiving preference work while they play.

Home Applications

Some children separate work and play, while others must combine the two activities. This is one area in which adults' awareness of preferences can have a great impact. For example, a parent might ask a child with a judging preference to do the dishes. The child is likely to complete the task as quickly as possible so that there will be plenty of time for fun activities. Children with this preference like to bring closure to tasks quickly. Parents with the same preference value this efficiency. The same cannot be said for the child with a perceiving prefer-ence. This child is more likely to prolong the task of doing the dishes by playing around. The sink might become a basketball hoop for the dishcloth. Drinking glasses might be stacked like a tower. Taking time to play with the soap bubbles might seem like a natural thing for the perceiving child to do. Some parents with a judging preference find this kind of behavior annoying. They cannot understand why the child doesn't complete the task and be done with it.

Parents may respond to such behavior by lecturing about the child's laziness, irresponsibility, or, at the very least, the child's in-competent way of performing a task. When the perceiving child responds by saying that it's important to have fun, some adults re-spond with, "Do you think work is going to be fun when you're out on your own? Get used to doing work as work and save play for play." Many children would find it discouraging to believe that life must be separated into work and play. As adults, many with perceiving preferences continue to incorporate work and play into a single activity and choose careers that enable them to do this.

One preference is not superior to another, but when a parent and child share different views, conflict often arises. Some parents with a judging preference have found it best to get the child to agree on the expected results, such as the kitchen being clean, for example. After making clear to the child what is expected, the parent should leave the area and not return until the task is complete. Usually the task will be completed no matter what the preference of the child, but the process of doing the task will be quite different according to preference. It is often the seemingly disorganized way that the perceiving child does things that seems to disturb the parent more than the quality of the results.

Judging children have a gift for planning ahead, while perceiving children have the gift of spontaneity.

School Applications

Each type has natural strengths and weaknesses. Children who learn about type learn how to work with their strengths and enhance their weaker skills, depending on the situation. Children who don't learn about type differences may try to emulate behaviors not suited to their strengths—just because the behavior worked well for someone else.

Students were asked to prepare a speech to present before the class. One child with a judging preference prepared note cards, practiced her presentation in front of a mirror, and planned how to present the speech effectively. On the day the students were to begin giving their presentations, this child asked someone with a perceiving preference if he was ready to give his speech. The perceiving child answered, "I guess so." When asked about the selected topic, the perceiving child answered, "I'm not really sure yet." The child with a judging preference felt more confident than ever that she was prepared.

When the time came to present the speeches, the child with a judging preference got up, gave an excellent speech, and got an A. When the child with a perceiving preference was called to give his speech, he got up, gave an excellent speech, and also got an A. The child with a judging preference said, "That's not fair. I worked hard and he didn't." The teacher had to explain that the grade was for the effectiveness of the presentation, not for the method of preparation. The child with a judging preference said, "Next time, I'm not going to plan and prepare either." But if the judging child took such action, she would be denying her natural talent to plan ahead and prepare. It just so happened that for this particular assignment, students could speak on any topic and the perceiving child therefore chose to speak about something he was familiar with. The gift of the perceiving child is spontaneity and flexibility. The student used his natural gifts and did well. The judging child used her natural gifts for planning and also did well. An awareness of type enables each child to recognize the best, most effective method for meeting task expectations. There will be assignments that require preparation that may run contrary to the natural gifts of perceiving children. In such instances, perceiving children cannot rely on their spontaneity to get them through the assignment. Then this child will need help planning and gathering information in a timely manner.

Understanding the needs of the different types can help explain certain behaviors.

Home Applications

When children with a judging preference have planned ahead, they do not appreciate other people ruining their plans. For example, a child with a judging preference was in a car pool with three friends. Their parents took turns driving. The children predetermined that they should be picked up at 7:30 A.M. One parent did not take the specificity of the pick-up time very seriously and therefore planned to arrive anytime between 7:35 and 7:45. His feeling was that the children would still get to school before the morning bell rang. But the child who had a judging preference was incredibly stressed by the delayed arrival of the driver. The children did get to school before the bell, but not in time to go to their lockers, meet with their friends, and prepare any last-minute details for class. This parent could not understand why the time factor was so important because, if he were in school, he would not need to arrive at school fifteen minutes before class started. Often adults impose their own emotional needs on children.

The child with a judging preference was put in a difficult position. The car pool was important, but it became stressful whenever this particular parent drove. Repeated attempts to encourage an earlier departure were ineffective because the adult was unable to understand the need to be there earlier. If he understood type differences, the child might be able to say, "I need to get to school fifteen minutes before class starts so I can organize my things and get ready for school. Can we please leave no later than 7:30?" The adult could respect the child's natural need to arrive at school early, accept this as a natural difference between them, and not make the child feel as though she needs to concoct a variety of reasons for being at school early.

Work and rest habits differ for judging and perceiving children.

Home Applications

The child with a judging preference feels pressured by a lot of tasks or assignments to be done simultaneously. Students who have three or four homework assignments in different subjects may stay up quite late trying to finish their work. One student was still studying for tests at midnight. His parent yelled, "Go to bed!" The child answered, "I can't. I'm not done yet." The parent *can* make the child go to bed but cannot help the child relax because children with a judging preference can't relax until their work is completed. If this child were to go to bed before finishing his schoolwork, he would in all likelihood lie awake worrying about the work he hadn't done.

Children with a perceiving preference do not share this concern about completing tasks. These children do better when they work at the last minute. The perceiving child is more apt to go to bed on time, then get up in the middle of the night or very early the next morning to complete an assignment.

If a parent has a difficult time understanding a child's preference, it is likely that the parent and child share different preferences. To better understand their child, the parent might ask some adult with the child's preference to describe how they preferred to do homework. When a parent is concerned about a child's habits, it is usually because the parent is afraid the habits are harmful, rude, or ineffective. If the child's style of completing homework does not disrupt anyone, is not making the child physically ill, and is getting the work done, then the style is effective for the child and the parent may need to develop a tolerance for this difference.

Judging children are task oriented in groups; perceiving children are process oriented.

School Applications

When students are grouped together for cooperative activities, the preference for judging or perceiving can have a significant impact on the way students function within the group. Children with a judging preference want to begin the assignment immediately and complete it as soon as possible, reflecting their strong need for closure. In contrast, students with a perceiving preference are inclined to explore all the possible avenues until time begins to run out. This tendency can cause them to act silly, discuss other topics, brainstorm improbable suggestions, and generally ignore the assignment. When the available time has almost elapsed, the group can gear into action. Such a situation is stimulating to perceivers but stressful for those with a judging preference. Similarly, perceiving types become stressed if they are given assignments that are completely defined and give them little or no options.

The writing styles of perceiving and judging children are different.

School Applications

One issue that relates to the judging and perceiving preference seems to occur with extended writing assignments. In a typical scenario, students are assigned a topic and asked to write a report. Once students are given all the information they need to begin preparing their reports, the judging students will select their references, organize the information, and begin to write. They complete the report. Teachers explain that they have a difficult time getting these students to rewrite first drafts because these students consider the first draft to be their final draft. Perceiving students, on the other hand, tend to gather more information than they can use for their report and delay putting their thoughts and ideas onto paper. The task for an instructor is to recognize that judging students will need different kinds of encouragement to rewrite their drafts and that perceiving students will need pacing to help them meet deadlines. Additional suggestions for working with such differences in working styles are detailed in Chapter 12, "Building Positive Relationships With Judging and Perceiving Children."

Summary

Judging and perceiving differences affect how people live together. An understanding of these characteristics can clarify the skills needed to be learned as well as the best path to teach these skills.

- Judging children seem to have an external order, while perceiving children seem to have an internal order.
- Tattletaling may provide young children with a way of determining whether a rule is still being enforced.
- Judgers work first, then play. Perceivers work while they play.

- Judging types plan ahead. Perceivers are flexible and spontaneous.

- Judgers must finish their work before they can rest. Perceivers rest first and then work at the last minute.

- Judging types are task oriented when they work in groups; perceiving types are process oriented.

- Judging children need encouragement to revise their writing, and perceiving children need encouragement to begin writing.

CHAPTER 7

■ ■

Applications of Type
to Parenting

Positive relationships are built on two primary sources. One source is shared experiences; the other is an appreciation of each individual's uniqueness.

Shared experiences are a base for relationships. Some parents and children live in the same home but never share experiences. Some divorced parents live far from their children, but distance does not determine whether experiences are shared. Experiences can be shared through direct or indirect contact, such as through phone conversations or mail correspondence. There must be some give and take in the interaction; contact cannot be one-sided. For there to be a shared experience, both parties must be involved in the experience.

The other primary source of establishing relationships, appreciating individual uniqueness, does not require both people to act and think alike. Two people can be completely different and still be able to value the insights and behaviors of the other person. Appreciation and toleration are distinguishably different. Frequently, one member of a relationship will say, "I've learned to live with this person. You can't change people." Learning to live with a characteristic or a behavior is not appreciating that difference, but tolerating it. Tolerating an individual difference does not contribute to the growth of a relationship, but appreciating a difference does. For a positive relationship to develop, both shared experiences and appreciation of individual differences must exist.

Adults have an inherent position of power over children.

When positive relationships are developing between children and parents, the position of power that parents hold over young children needs to be considered. Children, who must depend on adults for their survival, will always mentally recognize an emotional advantage that adults hold over children. Parental comments can be more powerful and have a stronger influence on children because of the power positions of parents. This perception of adult power begins to diminish when children enter adolescence, but it still exists to some extent. Some have questioned whether children today still view adults in positions of such power. Children can often project a sense of independence and may seem fearless of adults, but that does not mean that they perceive themselves as equals to adults. The words and actions of parents can greatly influence the thinking and behavior of children.

Understanding type differences can help parents recognize which of their children's behaviors are normal and which need correcting.

Parents and children will experience conflict at various times during children's developing years. Some parent-child problems cannot be easily resolved. Unhealthy elements within the family, such as alcoholism, can prevent parents and children from forming positive relationships through shared experiences and appreciating individual differences. Some parent-child conflict occurs naturally as children strive to find independence and become adults. Some conflict exists because parents and children do not understand and acknowledge the normal, healthy personality differences that exist among people. There is an expectation for their thoughts and feelings to be similar, and this expectation frames the definition of what is considered normal and acceptable. An unawareness of an insensitivity to the variation in normal personalities can prohibit parents from accepting some of the normal behaviors they find in their children. When normal differences are not understood, these unfamiliar behaviors have no validation. An awareness of type differences can help to explain why some parents discipline behaviors that other parents encourage. For example, two children from different families shared a similar type. Both were bold, spontaneous, and tried to create opportunities for new experiences. A friend of both children was a well-known golfer. Each child wanted to ask the golfer to take them golfing, even though neither had much experience with the game. One family said, "It never hurts to ask," and encouraged their child to approach the golfer with the request. The other family said, "Don't bother him. If he wants you to come, he'll ask you." These parents did not allow their child to approach the pro with the request. Each child followed a natural instinct. Each set of parents ran the behavior through the parents' filter and decided whether it was acceptable or not. An understanding of normal personality differences, then, can encourage the development of an appreciation of individual differences and contribute to the establishment of positive relationships between parents and children.

Environmental factors influence personality development but do not define it.

Some parents consider environmental influences to be the critical element shaping the total personality of their child. Philosophically, this position is referred to as the *blank slate* hypothesis. The blank slate hypothesis assumes that children are born as blank slates and that their personalities are shaped by the events that occur in their lives. Following this theory, a child can become anything, given the correct set of circumstances. Current theory suggests that personality preferences are more innate. The concept of a blank slate at birth denies inherent preferences. The concept of psychological type suggests that each child is born with a predisposition to personality preferences. These develop over an individual's lifetime. The development can be helped or hindered by events in the individual's lifetime. Therefore, environment affects development, but does not control the total personality.

Personality preferences according to psychological type are all normal, healthy differences that need to be cultivated.

Without type awareness, parents can project their impressions and perceptions upon their children.

Research supports the observation that most parents discipline their children the same way they were disciplined as children unless they have been taught alternative methods. Without an understanding of the natural differences in personality types, many adults will assume that their children experience situations the same way they did when they were children. Perhaps this explains why some parents want their children "to have the opportunities I never had" or "get the prom dress we could not afford." A parent's goal becomes superimposed on the child as if the child shared the same interpretation of events and held the same interests. Many adults try to remember their childhood as a strategy for making them more sensitive to the needs of their growing child. This process can be effective if the adult and child share the same personality preferences or if the adult limits the memories of their childhood to those that will help them address the child's basic developmental needs. Wickes (1966) emphasizes the impact that parental projections can have on child development. The child "is at the mercy of the psychology of the particular adult with whom he comes in contact" (p. 109). The expectations and perceptions of the adult shape a child's development. Unless there is an appreciation of different types, a parent can shape the child to resemble the parent's preferences rather than help to develop the child's natural preferences.

Children may falsify their type by imitating the preferences of the significant adults around them.

In some cases the personality of a parent or teacher can be overwhelming, and a child may feel compelled to imitate the adult pattern rather than express his or her own natural reactions. For instance, if a child has a preference for perceiving and feeling and the parent prefers judging, then the parent values behaviors such as planning ahead, being prepared, and reaching a conclusion. The parent appreciates when school projects are completed on time and when sufficient advance notice is given for school vacation days, fee deadlines, or teacher conferences. The parent expects the child to know how long assignments will take to complete, how to prepare the materials they will need, how to ask for necessary supplies well in advance, and how to work diligently at a task until it is completed. These expectations seem reasonable to the judging parent, but they are not typically characteristic of the perceiving child. Contrary to expectations of the judging parent, the perceiving child will want to keep all the available options open until the last minute, may easily forget to turn in assignments or bring home school notices, and will often want to gather supplies at the last minute. The child's feeling preference indicates that there is a strong need to be praised and valued at home. Parental feedback is extremely important to such children. If the parent is unable to respect the natural difference between the parent's judging style and the child's perceiving style, the parent can send a clear message to the child that the perceiving behaviors are not valued. In order to win parental approval, the child may begin to act like a judging child, although the natural preference of the child has not changed. Acting against natural preferences takes more energy and is stressful to the child, especially when a close bond exists between parent and child. Such a shift in the expression of preferences can inhibit the development of the child's natural preferences. Wickes (1966) explains that "such a confusion produces a sense of unreality and makes the integration of the personality a difficult task" (p. 110). The child cannot develop and integrate personal preferences when the child tries to imitate nonpreferred preferences.

Jung also addressed the power that the parent's personality can have on a child's developing personality. When the impact of the parental personality preference so strongly influences the child that the child begins to think and act like the parent, there is, over time, the possibility that the child will never develop the natural talents of his or her innate type and will present an outer personality that is opposed to his or her natural, inner preference. This falsification of type can become a serious source of emotional stress and can even be detrimental to a child's physiological well-being, leading to exhaustion (Jung, in Hull, 1971). The problem can be resolved by giving the child a chance to develop and express his or her natural preferences.

Honoring type differences is a way to show children they are loved and accepted.

How can parents know what to do or how to encourage the development of normal differences in their children? First, all children need to know they are loved and accepted. Normal development needs to proceed in a secure and loving environment. Otherwise the needs of the environment will hinder the child's developmental progress.

Honoring the developing differences in children and providing them with an environment that encourages exploration and the development of differences addresses their developmental needs. Parents can honor differences in two primary ways: The first is through their attitude; the second is through their actions. Bridging the gap between parents and children through attitude requires parents to accept the right of children to prefer a personality pattern different from their own. Bridging the gap through actions requires adults to proactively provide experiences in their children's worlds that enhance the development of their natural gifts.

Many parents may just want to know specifically what kinds of things will work with each child. There is no magic cookbook of answers, because each child is unquestionably an individual. Type can help explain natural preferences, but all the functions and attitudes described in the sixteen personality types can be found in each person and can be used in any situation. Type can help us understand behaviors we have observed and helps us define better ways to teach and communicate, but it does not predict behaviors.

Being aware of type differences does not mean people will necessarily enjoy these differences.

Some parents say they can understand the concept of normal, healthy differences but that they still find it difficult to live with their child on some days. Knowing about type differences may not make children's behaviors any easier to tolerate. If the parent values planning ahead, and the child continues to look for school supplies at the last minute, the parent may still become irritated with the child's lack of organization. Type can help determine which behaviors are easier for the child and which are more difficult. Type also explains how two siblings reared in the same environment can behave incredibly differently. Many parents reward children for developing the same skills and fail to recognize that the development of a particular skill requires different levels of energy and concentration for different children.

For example, one child in the family preferred judging and the other perceiving. Both were given keys to the house. Each day the child with a judging preference knew where to find the key. Each day the child with a perceiving preference had to look for the key. The perceiving child lost more than one house key. Parents who understand type understand that keeping track of a house key requires little effort for the judging child and much effort for the perceiving child. Expecting the task to be equal for both children is a denial of these inherent differences. Both can be expected to keep track of the key, but one child needs help learning the skill.

Children can also understand type differences.

Understanding type can help children understand their parents better. For instance, it may help them understand why their parents need some time alone or why their parents need to go out without them sometimes. Introverted adults, for example, are drained by constant communications throughout the day and value some quiet time to recharge so they can enjoy being with their children. Some introverted parents report that if they don't allow themselves this needed fifteen or so minutes of quiet and begin interacting immediately, tensions become high and many of their interactions with their children are negative. Children can better understand their parents' need for quiet time if they realize that there will later be time when their parents will listen to them.

Actions can speak louder than words.

Children learn from watching the behaviors of others, as can be evidenced from the following example. A family that was aware of type differences was composed of three introverts and one extravert. Over time, the extravert began to behave more introverted at home than in other environments. Even though the child had the emotional freedom and the verbal reinforcement to be extraverted, extraversion was never modeled in the home, while introversion was modeled daily. The child had no examples of the effective use of extraversion in the home and needed to look for examples of these behaviors elsewhere.

Parents cannot change their own preferences, but they can be sensitive to the needs of children whose preferences don't match their own or those of other children in the family. Part of bridging adult-child relationships is recognizing that a skill may be more natural for one sibling than for another. Parents who learn about and respect their children's rights to practice and improve a skill will build more positive relationships with their children than parents who expect a particular behavior in their children because other children the same age are able to do it. It is fair to expect all children to learn to do a particular task, but some flexibility should be allowed for how children with different types are taught to meet this goal.

Families can find their path to building positive relationships.

Later chapters will offer suggestions for interacting with children who have each of the sixteen personality types. Not all of the suggestions will work for all parents, because a parent's comfort with the suggestions will be influenced by his or her own type. In any relationship, the types of both people must be honored. Families can find their own path to developing positive relationships by developing attitudes and actions that honor the uniqueness of each family member.

Summary

Building positive relationships in families requires positive interactions and an appreciation of each person's individual differences. Type is a tool to clarify these differences.

- Building positive relationships between parents and children requires quality interactions and appreciation of each other's individual development.
- Adults have an inherent position of power over children.
- Understanding type differences helps us to know which behaviors are normal and which need correcting.
- Environmental factors influence personality development but do not define it.
- Without an awareness of type, parents can project their impressions and perceptions on children.
- Children may falsify type by imitating the preferences of adults who are significant to them.
- Operating in types opposite one's natural preference can be exhausting and stressful.
- Positive relationships between adults and children can be achieved through attitudes and actions.
- Honoring type differences can help meet the need of children to know they are loved and accepted.
- Being aware of type differences does not necessarily mean that people will enjoy these differences.

- An awareness of type can also help children understand the behaviors of their parents.

- Modeled behaviors can be as powerful an influence on children as verbal reinforcement of behaviors.

- In any relationship, the types of both people must be honored.

Chapter 8

■ ■

Applications of Type
to Teaching

There are at least as many applications of type in the school setting as there are in the home because, just as is the case for families, successful results depend on the development of positive relationships between teachers and children. The importance of teachers understanding the concept of personality type differences cannot be understated. When teachers understand type differences, it can influence how they present lessons, how they construct tests, and how they design classroom rules. Teaching in a way that honors the different processing styles should result in higher achievement. Additionally, the classroom should become a more pleasant environment for teachers and students.

The type preferences of teachers influences their instructional presentation designs.

Multiple workshops were conducted with groups of teachers. During training activities, teachers were divided into two groups according to their preferences for sensing or intuition and asked to design a reading lesson that would teach students three vocabulary terms. Teachers were told that the students would be expected to read the new words, then define and use them in a new context. The two groups' lesson designs were then compared.

Sensing teachers frequently chose methods of introducing each word and examining the letters, sound, syllabication, and mechanics for phonetic analysis. These teachers then planned to introduce a definition for each term. Next, the students were expected to determine which of the three words fit into prewritten sentences. Finally, the students were asked to compose three new sentences using each of the terms.

Intuitive teachers listening to the sensing teachers design the reading lesson frequently reported that they found the lesson boring and would not feel motivated to do the tasks. The intuitive teachers' lesson designs almost always began with a story or theme relating the three terms. In one instance, the selected terms were *exquisite, barrister,* and *maze.* Intuitive teachers designed a story about an exquisite princess who was trapped in a tower. The prince in the story had to work his way through a maze in order to recover the trapped princess. After her release, the princess' captor had to face charges in court and needed the services of a barrister to help with his defense. The stories were elaborate and frequently used the target words. However, no actual definition of the words was offered. The students would be expected to glean the meaning of the terms from the context of the multiple examples offered. This is something that intuitive children can accomplish more easily than sensing children.

The designed activities were later shared with groups of students. Sensing students listening to the intuitive teachers' lesson stated that the activity sounded fun but wondered when the lesson would finally be taught. Sensing children responded to the intuitive teachers' lesson by saying that they didn't know what meaning to ascribe to the words and that the story had so many words in it that by the end they weren't even sure which words they were expected to study. Intuitive children, in contrast, loved the intuitive teachers' lesson design. When given the lesson designed by sensing teachers, these children thought the work was boring.

Most teaching lessons are designed in the style of the teacher. Sensing children respond well to the sequential introduction of material typically used by sensing teachers, and intuitive children respond well to the method of introducing global themes typically used by intuitive teachers. Teaching lessons do not all necessarily need to be designed in the style of the learner, but it's important to keep in mind that in many classrooms, children whose types are different from the teacher may never have their preferences addressed in teaching lessons. Teachers who use a knowledge of type to honor the natural differences developing in children are able to balance their teaching lessons so that the learning preferences of all types can be respected.

Type preferences of teachers can affect their design of test questions.

Test questions are typically designed as multiple choice, matching, short answer, short essay, or long essay. There are other ways to assess whether learning has occurred, but the test question format seems to be used most frequently.

In another training activity, teachers were divided into four groups instead of two. The groups were arranged according to the teacher's dominant function preference—sensing, intuition, thinking, or feeling. The groups were given the task of assuming that their classes had just completed an intensive course in drug prevention awareness. Teachers were then asked to design three test questions to assess their students' level of learning. Each group designed different questions and, in the discussions that ensued about the questions, often stated that they would have a difficult time answering or grading the questions other groups developed. Examples of the different styles of questions designed by the groups are shown in Figure 7.

These questions reflect the different ways that teachers with different personality types design test questions. This activity was repeated at least twenty times, and groups arranged by type consistently designed similar questions. Sensing teachers focus on the details of the information they present to students, intuitive teachers design broad essay questions, thinking teachers focus on why and punishment issues, and feeling teachers design questions that revolve around the way things affect people. The natural differences of adults who have different preferences are reflected in the types of questions designed. The important thing to remember is that children of all types will take tests designed by

Figure 7. Test Question Design by Type

Sensing Preference

1. List 3 reasons why people try drugs:
    a.
    b.
    c.
2. Name and describe the major classifications of drugs and their effects on the human body.
3. Give an example of how drugs may have had adverse effects on the life of someone famous.

Intuitive Preference
1. Is the war on drugs succeeding? Why or why not? 2. If you were the President of the United States, what would you do to help America's youth? 3. In essay form, design three questions and explain why these would cover the material.

Thinking Preference
1. Why say no to drugs? 2. Should drugs be legalized? Why or why not? Be prepared to support your answer. 3. How would you punish the drug-pushers?

Feeling Preference
1. How could you persuade your best friend to say no to drugs? 2. What do you feel society should/could do to win the war against drugs? 3. How does drug abuse affect the entire family?

a teacher who is of one particular type. Teachers who make an effort to balance their tests with a variety of questions that honor the different types of all students find that their students demonstrate greater achievement. These students don't necessarily study more; their teachers simply find better ways to let them demonstrate what they have learned.

Type differences can have an impact on classroom rules.

Classroom atmosphere is also naturally shaped by the type preference of the teacher. This can create problems when a child's type is different from the teacher's type. An example observed in one school may help to clarify this point. Once a group of students were observed as they went from one classroom to another. In the first class, students sat perfectly still, raised their hands to speak, spoke only enough to answer the teacher's question, and made no extraneous noises. Some students in the class were focused and interested, but others were bored and inattentive. At the end of the class period, the students got up, walked twenty feet to get to their next class, and suddenly behaved differently, seeming to become different students. The students all seemed to be talking. They were more casual in their posture. During the discussion of a social studies topic, many students carried on other discussions or called out their interesting ideas. Students were nodding and actively involved in generating ideas from other students' contributions. The noise level in the classroom was high, as was the energy level of the students. When the class was asked to complete a worksheet on the topic, some worked in teams and some tried to work alone. Some students found the class stimulating, but others had difficulty finding a place where they could concentrate to complete the assignment. Each of the two classroom environments more closely matched the learning preference of the teacher, and in each some children were attentive and some were stressed. Type can help explain the different needs of students as something that is completely unrelated to ability, effort, or motivation.

Wait time is not the same for extraverts and introverts.

The time that teachers allow students to collect their thoughts before answering a question relates to the way the teacher prefers to interact with the world, either through extraversion or introversion. In one study, an introverted and an extraverted teacher each observed the other teaching a lesson. At the conclusion of the lesson, the teachers were asked if they felt they allowed students sufficient wait time before they were expected to answer questions. Both felt they did. The extraverted teacher was asked if the introverted teacher provided enough wait time. The teacher responded, "Way too much time was left. The lesson began to drag, and some of the children were getting bored." The introverted teacher was asked if the extraverted teacher provided enough wait time. The teacher answered, "No. Too fast. The kids had no time to think through carefully." Both teachers measured the quality of the wait time that the other provided on their teaching preference and not on the learning preferences of the students.

Teachers can sometimes judge children's performance based on personalized systems.

Teachers form many judgments about a student's level of class participation. Frequently, teachers are asked to evaluate how well students participate in class discussions. Extraverted and introverted teachers may respond differently to the same behaviors in students, as is evidenced by the following example.

One extraverted teacher was asked to lead a group discussion on a selected topic. Twenty minutes into the discussion, the teacher was asked to determine how well each student was participating in the discussion. The extraverted teacher went around the room and identified the students who participated: "She did because she said something, and he nodded, and she spoke, and she gave me eye contact, and he gave his opinion." The teacher then continued by identifying the students who did not participate: "But she didn't and he didn't, and neither did she."

The students who were identified as noncontributors were asked how they felt about the way the teacher viewed them. Most were angry that the teacher had inferred that they were not participating. Each understood the content of the discussion but had not formulated their thoughts fully enough to share them with others. Some of the students who were identified as participators admitted that after they had made their contribution they stopped listening to the discussion. Chances are that if the extraverted teacher were involved in a group discussion, she would speak, give eye contact, nod, and show external behaviors that clearly said, "I am involved," and this was what the teacher expected of others to show their level of participation. However, because she did not understand introversion, she misjudged the introverted students' level of participation. If a teacher wants to accurately determine whether students are participating in a discussion, judgments should not be made on the basis of overt behaviors. At the conclusion of a class discussion, teachers can ask students to write three or four statements that reflect what they learned from the discussion. If students can demonstrate that they learned the material by doing this, then they participated in the discussion whether they made comments to the group or not. Of course, if the learning objective is to speak before a group, then this suggestion is ineffective. But it can be applied to most classroom discussions, which focus on the retention of topic information, not on oral delivery skills.

Debriefing is a strategy that honors all types.

Debriefing is a process that allows teachers to address the needs of all types after a group discussion. If the students are aware of type differences, the teacher can use type terms. If the students are not aware of type terms, the teacher can use examples. Both approaches will have a similar impact. In the course of any well-designed discussion, the needs of each of the different functions—sensing, intuition, thinking, and feeling—should be addressed. Examples of statements made throughout the discussion can later be used in the review of the discussion. For our purposes, let's assume that a group is discussing environmental problems. At the conclusion of the discussion, the teacher might say, "Let's review some key points from our discussion. Jim, thank you for your clear presentation of the problems associated with air pollution. We understand auto emission better because of the rich details you included. Jane, thank you for helping us get a better focus of how environmental issues impact other issues. Your statement that linked recycling paper to the destruction of the rain forests helped us get a better total picture of that whole issue. John, thank you for your comments about the need to organize all countries to limit the levels of fluorocarbons they release into the atmosphere in order to minimize damage to the ozone layer. Jill, thank you for bringing our focus to people and how each person can help solve environmental problems." If students had knowledge of type terminology, the teacher could have said, "Jim, thank you for the sensing perspective that included such rich details on auto emissions. Jane, thank you for the intuitive perspective that helps us tie each of the pieces together to see the total picture. John, thank you for your thinking perspective that presents how systems work together logically to solve a common problem, and Jill, thank you for the feeling perspective that brings the focus of the problems to the daily lives of the people involved." The students do not necessarily need to be aware of type differences to honor the different thinking styles, but the teacher does. Although only four students were recognized for their contributions, other students who shared those perspectives feel that their ideas are affirmed as well. This kind of review takes about a minute, but the impact can be phenomenal. Too often in group discussions, the focus veers to the preference of the teacher because the teacher inadvertently sends signals back to the class that a particular focus is more important or more appreciated. Teachers who make an effort to recognize the contributions of students who exemplify each of the functions are less likely to limit the discussion to their preferred style. Teachers who would like to review class discussions based on type differences should look for:

- Specifics and details to recognize the sensing perspective
- Themes and global statements to recognize the intuitive perspective

- Systems and organization to recognize the thinking perspective
- Issues relevant to service to people and impact on people to recognize the feeling perspective

Type influences the way teachers teach.

The teacher's type preferences influence how information is presented, how lessons are designed, and how classroom rules are devised. The student's type preferences influence how information is received and how information is shared. The process of teaching and learning involves a relationship between teachers and students, and the more that can be done to promote healthy relationships between the two, the more learning can occur. One way to build healthy relationships between adults and children is for adults, including parents and teachers, to recognize that a skill that one child needs to learn may come naturally to another child. The teacher who is aware of and respects a child's right to practice and improve a skill will build a more positive relationship with the child than the teacher who expects a particular behavior just because other children the same age can meet that expectation.

Type should never be used as an excuse for not meeting educational expectations.

When teachers first learn about type, the question that frequently arises is whether it is fair to expect certain types to do particular assignments. If an assignment is well designed and has a clear instructional goal, then *all* students should be expected to complete it. The way a teacher helps students reach a goal may differ according to the different personality types of the children, but the expectation for students to meet the goal should not. Type should never be used as an excuse to explain why a student fails to meet an educational expectation. Type awareness can help ensure that educational expectations are appropriate and fair for all children.

Language can be used to honor the developing preferences of children.

Once teachers and students are aware of type, it can be tempting to assign students to work in groups according to their preferences for extraversion or introversion, sensing or intuition, or any other pair of type preferences. This approach implies that children have only one preference or the other. In reality, each person *possesses* all of the sixteen preferences, but *develops* preferences for only some of them. When groups are being formed, it is better to offer children a choice: "Those who want to use their sensing skills can work here. Those who want to use their intuitive skills can work there." This process acknowledges that the other skill exists and may be used at another time and in another situation. Recognizing the presence of all functions is especially important for young children who are still developing a dominant function. They must be given opportunities to practice using all the functions in order to develop a preference for one.

If the teacher understands type differences but the students have not been introduced to the topic, the teacher can still allow students to make choices by describing activities instead of using type vocabulary terms such as sensing and intuition to identify them. For example, students who are going to work on a hypothetical problem about living in space would not need to be assigned to sensing and intuitive groups. Instead, the teacher could define the groups according to task: "Those of you who would like to generate a list of the most important supplies to take with you to space can work here (sensing). Those of you who would like to brainstorm about where to travel in space and what experiments to research can work there (intuition)." The students would naturally choose to be in the group that would be doing the kind of activity that appealed to them the most on that particular day. Children who choose a sensing task one day might just as easily choose an intuitive task another day without realizing that choosing different tasks provides them with practice using different functions and enables them to develop a dominant preference.

Teachers can utilize the strengths of other teachers.

Teachers cannot be expected to learn everything there is to know about each of the sixteen types. Teachers will naturally understand students who have preferences similar to their own and must make an effort to learn the gifts of those who have opposite preferences. If the teacher wants to develop directions that both sensing and intuitive students can easily understand, he or she can make a draft version of the directions and then ask another teacher who has an opposite preference to review them and make corrections. Intuitive teachers may find that sensing teachers help clarify points that they didn't think needed to be stated, and sensing teachers may find that intuitive teachers can help them broaden the topic to include a greater wealth of possibilities. Teamwork with other teachers who have opposite preferences will strengthen lesson designs and assessment tools by making use of the natural strengths of opposite preferences.

Type differences can be honored in all educational settings.

Many innovations are offered to educators as tools to improve instructional effectiveness. Type awareness has specific strengths that make it an easy tool for teachers to acquire and implement. First, it requires no change in curriculum goals or areas of concentration. The concepts focus on teaching and learning styles and not on lesson content. Teachers who are aware of type differences but do not know their content field may be able to create a pleasant learning environment, but their students will not do well on achievement tests in that subject area. Type awareness does not replace the good teaching strategies that teachers already practice. Type can enhance the effective use of teaching strategies and provide a template for designing additional strategies that transcend all content fields.

Using type concepts does not introduce additional paperwork for the teacher. Teachers must still prepare teaching lessons and design assessment tools. How these are designed may be modified, but using type theory in educational settings does not inherently create more administrative work.

Bridging student-teacher relationships by developing a clearer perspective of student behavior influences the perception of those behaviors. Teachers who previously labeled the behaviors of perceiving students as irresponsible or lazy may now be able to recognize these as behaviors demonstrated by students who have difficulty working against deadlines and will thus respond to the students differently. Viewing the perceiver's behavior as irresponsible or lazy implies that the student needs an attitude adjustment, whereas the latter interpretation implies that the student needs some guidance formulating timelines. It is easier and more productive to teach a student how to develop a timeline than it is to attempt to adjust an attitude.

Finally, type does not need to be introduced into education all at once. It can be done in stages. First, teachers should become familiar with their personality preferences and explore how these preferences affect their teaching style. Second, teachers can learn to work with other teachers to develop lessons and tests that honor the type differences of students. Third, students can be introduced to type concepts as a strategy to help them learn more about their strengths and their learning needs. Introducing students to type has the added benefit of helping them understand the needs of students with other types, and the instructional style of the teacher. Students and teachers can learn to accommodate each other based on specific situational demands, and type can help provide the framework for understanding these needs.

Summary

Type differences have an impact on the learning environment. Teachers who develop an awareness of type discover a tool to promote learning while honoring individual differences.

- Presentations of lessons, the design of assessment tools, and classroom procedures are all influenced by the type preferences of teachers.

- Reviewing discussions provides one strategy for honoring the different processing styles of students.

- Type should *never* be used as an excuse for failing to meet an educational expectation.

- Teachers should allow students to choose which group they would like to work in on a particular day based on activity rather than assign students to groups based on projected type preferences.

- Teachers who confer with teachers who have opposite preferences can improve the quality of their presentations and assessment tools so that they honor the different learning styles of children.

- Type is a strategy for improving education that does not change content fields, produce additional paperwork, or require that changes be made rapidly.

■ ■

Chapter 9

Building Positive Relationships With Introverted and Extraverted Children

This chapter contains suggestions for building positive relationships between adults and children based on the extraverted or introverted needs of each person. Each child is a unique individual, so the suggestions offered here may not be appropriate for every child. Use the suggestions that work, modify the ones that don't, or design new strategies to meet the needs of individual children based on an understanding of type differences.

Parents' preferences can influence how children's reactions are perceived.

Home Applications

Extraverted children deal with their feelings through verbal expression. This means that they may yell back when they are angry. Some introverted parents have a difficult time accepting this. It is easier for them to understand children who get upset and run to the privacy of their bedroom than it is for them to understand children who want to remain in a situation and become confrontational. Extraverted parents, in contrast, have stated that they don't believe it is right for children to avoid confrontation by retreating to their rooms, and often ask children to stay and settle an issue by talking it through right then and there. Introverted children are not only uncomfortable in such situations; they are often unable to talk about their feelings when they are angry. These children tend to draw inward to resolve their feelings with themselves before they are able to discuss them with others.

Extraverted children tend to state their feelings the instant they feel them. Some introverted parents have found that extraverted children do not always need someone to respond to their comments. Allowing children to have the space to verbally express their negative feelings does not mean that you necessarily agree with their feelings, but it does recognize that different personality types deal with anger and frustration differently. When the type preference of the child matches that of the parent, it is easier for the parent to understand the child's behaviors. Understanding the behaviors of a child who has a different preference can help build better adult-child relationships.

Ask extraverted children to wait briefly before beginning a conversation with an introverted adult.

Home and School Applications

Extraverted children seem to assume that if nothing is visibly happening in the outside world, then nothing is happening. Introverted adults may appear not to be doing anything, but their minds may be racing a mile a minute over a particular problem or idea. Extraverted children may perceive that an adult isn't doing anything and tend to come into the room where the adult is and instantly begin talking. Because introverts dislike interruptions, the tendency is for the adult to say, "What? What did you say? What is it that you want?" The tone does not indicate to the child that a conversation is invited. The child responds to the tone and says, "Never mind. Why are you so grouchy?" In circumstances like this, some children will walk away and a gap will develop in their relationship with the adult.

One strategy that works with some extraverted children is establishing a rule that once the child calls the parent or the teacher's name, no conversation can begin until the child counts to ten. This allows the introverted adult enough time to put aside previous thoughts and focus exclusively on the child's information or question. The awareness that extraverts and introverts process thoughts differently respects this rule because it does not suggest that the introvert is not interested in what the extravert has to say; it just recognizes the introvert's need to close one thought before becoming receptive to new ones. The concept of adults changing "channels" so they can listen better is something young children can understand. Telling the child something along the lines of, "By the time you count to ten I can change my thinking channel to a listening channel so I can hear you better," is something children can understand, and children don't mind following rules if they understand them.

"Show time" provides children with the opportunity to share.

One concept that works with many families and classes is something called *show time*. Ten to fifteen minutes are set aside for sharing. In classrooms, this can be scheduled near the end of the school day or prior to lunch or recess. At home, time can be set aside each evening (or each week, if that is how frequently the child sees the parent). At the selected time, the class or the parent gives the child undivided time and attention.

Home Applications

Most families try to communicate while doing several other things, such as reading the paper, preparing dinner, working, or helping a sibling. When children are given ample time with their parents, many find that they can't think of anything to do or talk about that takes up the scheduled ten to fifteen minutes. Initially, children complete their show time in two or three minutes. This is because the family's communication pattern has been for family members to exchange three or four sentences and then part company. In fifteen minutes, a child can share many aspects of him or herself. During time that is recognized as show time, it is extremely important for parents not to accept phone calls, speak about other things, or do anything that can be done at another time. The fifteen minutes should belong to the child. If children can count on having this time to share, they have little need to immediately bombard parents with their thoughts and problems when their parents first return home from work.

School Applications

In the classroom, show time has provided class comedians with opportunities to shine. If children begin to clown around in class, the teacher can schedule a performance for three or so minutes and ask the students to prepare a routine. A student can give the performance on that day or later in the week, but no more time than a week should elapse from the time of the child's performance-like behavior. Daily performances don't have to be planned, but some teachers prefer to allow three minutes disciplining disruptive behavior rather than providing three minutes as a vehicle for this kind of behavior to occur. Knowing that the option of having performance time is available may be enough to deter some students from disrupting the class.

Extraverts need to become known after they move to a new school, while introverts may appreciate a peer-buddy to help them get acquainted.

School Applications

Children often move frequently and must therefore be able to adjust to different instructional settings. Forming friendships can be difficult for children who repeatedly change schools. Because extraverted children are so outgoing and friendly, it may seem that they may have fewer problems adjusting to school changes, but this assumption may be misleading. Adults should understand how important it is to extraverted children for other children to know them. How can they, for example, be invited to a friend's house, called on the phone, or asked to join a game if no one knows their name? It isn't the number of children the extraverted child knows that is important, but the number of other people who know the extraverted child. One extravert reported that the best thing that happened to her after she moved and began attending a new school was that the principal asked her to read a story to each of the classes. After that, many of the other students knew her name, called her, and she felt like she belonged. An introverted child would probably not find this strategy an effective way to help adjust to a move. For the introverted child, having a peer-buddy to meet at the door each day, have lunch with, and ask questions of would be more helpful. This peer-buddy should be appointed by the teacher or the counselor. The introvert should not be expected to make this selection. An extravert may be a good peer-buddy because the extravert is likely to take the student to many groups within the class. This peer-buddy relationship might officially last for two weeks at least. Two weeks gives the introvert time to acclimate to new people. After two weeks, the relationship can continue if both want it to continue. Letting extraverts have opportunities for involvement with others and letting introverts enter a new school and make new friends at a more cautious pace is a way of honoring type differences.

Adults can teach extraverts how to retain their thoughts while they wait to be called on.

Young extraverted children have a difficult time keeping their thoughts to themselves until it is their turn to talk. When extraverted children are asked to wait their turn to talk, and then a few moments later are given an opportunity to talk, they often state that they have forgotten what they were going to say. These children may not remember their thoughts, but their need to share their ideas is a real one. Young extraverted children need to be taught how to retain their thoughts until they have an opportunity to share them with others.

School Applications

If the child has strong visualization skills, it might help to have the child create a mental picture of the activity he or she wants to describe. That picture can keep the thought alive by making it active and moving. However, children younger than second grade may find it difficult to form visualizations. It might help these children to try repeating to themselves one main word that will help them remember what they want to say. In the classroom, these extraverted children might call out answers and want to share frequently. In the school setting, children can also jot down a word or phrase, or draw a picture to help them remember their thoughts. Some extraverts may come from families where it is acceptable for several people to talk at the same time during dinner, but some introverted families may consider it rude for children to burst into a conversation with their ideas.

Home and School Applications

Sometimes children are disciplined for interrupting conversations. Extraverted children are so drawn into the world and engage in all the activity around them that keeping their thoughts active while others are talking is difficult. Adults who appreciate this difference will understand that telling introverted children to "wait a moment" before talking is not the same as telling extraverted children to do the same. This doesn't mean that adults should allow children to make interruptions if they consider them unacceptable. However, it is more appropriate to teach them how to redirect themselves than to discipline their natural needs. The ability of children to retain thoughts will develop over time. Telling young extraverted children not to make interruptions without providing them with a strategy for keeping their ideas active is placing the children at a disadvantage in the conversation. The behaviors adults choose to redirect or discipline often depend not only on the child's natural preference but also on the preferences of the adults.

Extraverted adults can overwhelm introverted children with their high energy levels.

Home and School Applications

Extraverted adults can overwhelm introverted children with their energy levels. Many extraverted adults, in their efforts to encourage introverted children to talk, ask multiple questions, ask probing questions, and allow very little wait time between questions for children to answer. The extraverts' high energy can seem like an ocean wave that swallows up the introvert. Instead of encouraging conversation, the questions and probes of the extraverted adult actually discourage conversation. Several tactics can help foster communication. Adults can try phrasing questions so that children cannot answer with single words or short phrases. Adults can avoid asking questions that can be answered with short responses like "Yes," "No," "Red," or "Pizza," for example. They can instead try to ask open-ended questions that encourage longer, more revealing answers. Instead of asking, "How was school today?" adults can ask, "Tell me what you did in school today." They can then provide the child with sufficient time to answer the question. Because wait times are different for extraverts and introverts, an extraverted adult may interrupt the thinking process of an introverted child by posing additional questions or prompts. An alternative is to try and enjoy the quiet times in a conversation. The silence is perceived only by the extravert because the mind of the introvert may be racing with thoughts. When in doubt, extraverts can always ask, "Would you like a little more time to think before answering?

Instead of questioning and probing, an extraverted adult might maintain communication with an introverted child by talking to the child without asking questions. This works especially well at the end of a long day when the child is tired. The parent can talk about the day and allow the child to just listen. If the parent shares one or two thoughts and then waits for five or ten seconds, the introverted child may also begin to share. Introverted children are not likely to interrupt someone who is talking, so the quiet time provides a necessary door-opener for introverts who are ready to share. If the child makes no comment during pauses in the conversation, the parent can share two more things about the day. Parents who tell their children about the day's activities share a part of themselves that increases the awareness that parents and children have of each other and contributes to a growing album of shared experiences. It's important to keep in mind that the child may enjoy hearing about the parent's world as much as the parent enjoys hearing about the child's. Knowledge of each other's daily experiences helps to build positive adult-child relationships.

Some introverted children need time to recharge their energy levels after a period of interacting.

Home Applications

The introvert's need for "down time" can potentially be viewed as a sign of a communication problem between parents and children. One extraverted parent, for example, had two adopted children. One of the children was an extravert and the other was an introvert. When the parent took the extravert to after-school activities, they chatted about all the events of the day, what they would have for dinner, what was going to be on TV that night, and anything else they felt like talking about. When the parent took the introvert to after-school activities, the parent found herself doing a lot of questioning but getting very limited answers in return. She was concerned that she and the introverted child were not bonding properly. In fact, the introverted child had just spent a full day at school and was now going to dance class. School and after-school activities require extraverted participation. The only opportunity the child had to relax and recharge her energy level was during the car ride between school and the activities. In this case, the silence during the car ride had nothing to do with the parent-child bond, but rather the introvert's need for some time to re-energize. Knowing about type preferences can help adults distinguish perceived problems from genuine ones.

Introverts and extraverts express thoughts at different times.

Home Applications

Introverted parents may tend to overreact to the comments of extraverted children. Extraverted children are likely to express whatever thoughts come into their heads. For example, an extraverted child might casually say, "I think I am going to drop out of school." An introverted parent might overreact and begin lecturing the child about why she should remain in school. Before long the child is defending her right to make her own decisions and drop out if that is her choice. By overreacting to an initial statement, the parent made the child defend a statement that may not have been the child's final thought. Sometimes letting extraverted children talk through their ideas until their final thoughts are formed can reveal different issues than the initial statement suggested. The extraverted child might have said something like, "I think I'll quit school. I mean, why should I keep going back to a place where everyone is so stupid? Do you know what they want us to do tonight? We have to cut out pictures from magazines. Isn't that ridiculous? Why should we have to find the visuals? I'll bet the teacher is just too lazy to do the job, and that's why we have to cut out stupid pictures. I don't even think we have any magazines with pictures of the environment. I mean, I guess I could look at some of those old *Time* and *Newsweek* magazines we have upstairs, but it's still a dumb thing to have to do. I guess I'll do it while I watch 'The Simpsons'." It's important to let extraverted children talk through an issue. Extraverted parents may naturally allow for this thought process to be completed, since they would follow a similar process. It is important to recognize that most disciplinary situations result from the interaction of the parent's preference and the child's preference and not solely from the child's dilemma.

Extraverts and introverts express anger differently.

Home Applications

Many adults who live and work with extraverted children are faced with a difficult choice. Extraverts can deal with feelings of anger by expressing them. This means that it is quite possible for an extraverted child to yell back to a parent in a way that an introvert would not. The introverted child may have the same kind of angry thoughts that the extraverted child expresses. Parents should realize that just because they don't hear the thoughts doesn't mean that they don't exist. Parents of infants who have observed older children yelling at their parents may have said, "My child will never talk to me that way." But they may later find themselves faced with a child who does just that. When possible, parents need to separate yelling from disrespectful behavior. Not many angry children are able to express their anger in a quiet way, so loudness naturally accompanies the expression of anger. Allowing children to vent their true feelings is quite different from allowing them to behave disrespectfully or rudely.

Neither disrespect nor rudeness are related in any way to type preferences. If you are an adult who is dealing with an extraverted child who yells, try to stay calm. Allow the child to speak briefly, and then ask if he or she is ready to bring the volume down and discuss the situation. An old cartoon caption read something to the effect that parents are most dangerous when they positively, absolutely, refuse to get angry.... If remaining calm is too difficult, try separating yourself from the situation. Say something like, "I'm too angry to discuss this now. I'll talk to you after dinner." Be sure to give a specific time. Just saying "later" will mean nothing to the child.

Some introverted children become so angry that they will leave the room. Then when they calm down, they often do not know how to begin to apologize or start a conversation with their parents. Sometimes several days will pass before older introverted children are able to calmly discuss an issue. Some families find it effective to use a symbol to indicate when family members are ready to talk. The symbol should be agreed on during calm periods. Symbols might be written notes, a touch, performing something nice, or anything mutually agreeable to adults and children. One family uses magnets with happy and sad faces. If the sad face is on, discussions are off. When the face changes to the happy face, the child or the adult is ready to talk. Each family member has a magnet face to use.

Different approaches can help improve test achievement.

School Applications

One teacher decided to initiate a strategy to help improve the quality of essay responses on tests. Tests were distributed, and the students read the essay choices. Students then had to wait approximately ten minutes before they could begin answering the questions. During the ten minutes, the students could process their thoughts individually, or they could discuss their ideas with other students. Sections of the room were divided for each group. At the end of the ten minutes, all the students wrote individually, and the quality of their essay answers improved over previous tests. If talking helps organize thoughts, allowing that process to occur during assessment as well as instruction can enhance students' abilities to effectively present ideas. Ten minutes in a group conversation is not going to "give someone the answers" to an essay question, but it can facilitate the organization and effective expression of answers.

"Conversation sticks" are one way to encourage participation.

School Applications

Teachers of young children can use *conversation sticks* to help encourage introverts to participate and encourage extraverts to hold on to their ideas. To use this strategy, give children two popsicle sticks (or whatever other token is available), and each time a child shares an idea or a piece of information, have that child give you one of the tokens. Once a child spends all of his or her tokens, he or she cannot share again until *all* the children in the class have spent their tokens. The teacher can then reissue another set of tokens if he or she wishes. This strategy is good for language groups or group discussions where participation by all members is important. The group should remain small—six students is a large group to a kindergarten child. Classes can be divided into teams of four to six students, and each team can use the conversation sticks. Every team can discuss the same topic, but limiting the number of members can increase the opportunities for both introverts and extraverts to share.

Cooperative teams can give all children a chance to express their ideas.

School Applications

Sometimes it helps to group students into cooperative teams of two or four. The teacher then asks the class a question. Students are not allowed to answer the question without first checking with their teammates. This strategy allows all children to express their thoughts; it affirms the value of talking with peers; and it offers a chance for students to initiate new friendships. Extraverted students who are given this opportunity to talk with peers about instructional information are given the chance to form their thoughts before they express them to the entire class.

Expectations for student participation can revolve around a lesson's objective.

School Applications

If a class of 25 or more students is expected to carry on a conversation about a selected topic, the teacher must weigh the importance of having each student contribute to the discussion against the importance of covering all the key points of the topic. Requiring all students to share implies that the primary goal of the discussion is to provide students with an opportunity to practice their expressive skills before a group. Allowing students who want to speak to volunteer implies that thoughts about the discussion topic are more important than the identity of the person expressing them. If information is the focus of the lesson, teachers can write on the class chalkboard: "Share by choice."

This means that students have the choice of sharing. If development of expressive skills is the objective of the lesson, teachers can write on the chalkboard: "All share." This lets students know that they are expected to contribute. Some introverts would rather volunteer early than wait to be called on. Again, teachers can measure the participation of all students by asking every student to write three or four things they gleaned from the group discussion. This allows the teacher to evaluate class participation based on the comprehension level of the students and not on the level of overt involvement in the discussion.

This chapter has discussed a sample of strategies that can help improve relationships with introverted or extraverted children. Many other strategies are possible. Understanding, or bridging by attitude, is the first step to building positive relationships. Activities, or bridging by action, is the second step.

Summary

Numerous strategies are effective tools for honoring extraverted and introverted preferences. Many of these can be used in the home and in the school.

- Activities energize the extraverted child, while interactions with others can exhaust the introverted child.
- Extraverted children tend to argue and express feelings of anger, while introverted children tend to keep their feelings to themselves.
- Extraverted children do not realize when they are interrupting the thoughts of introverted adults. Asking extraverted children to pause briefly before they begin speaking helps.
- "Show time" allows children to interact with adults at scheduled times and promotes appreciation of differences.
- Extraverts and introverts who move to new schools may need different adjustment strategies.
- It helps to teach extraverts strategies for keeping their ideas alive while others are given a chance to share.

- The behaviors adults choose to redirect or discipline are influenced by their type preferences; often it is the interaction of the adult's and the child's type preferences that generate misunderstandings.

- To draw an introverted child into a conversation, talk to the child instead of asking questions. Pause between statements to allow an opening for the introvert to talk.

- Silence is not necessarily an indication of a relationship or communication problem.

- Allowing students some time to discuss or ponder test questions may improve the quality of their essay answers.

- Conversation sticks can help structure small group discussions for young children.

- Using cooperative learning strategies gives extraverts and introverts opportunities to share in small groups when opportunities to share with the entire class are limited.

- Teachers can choose to allow students to share by choice or require that all share, depending on the objective of the lesson.

CHAPTER 10

■ ■

Building Positive Relationships With Sensing and Intuitive Children

Sensing and intuition focus on the way people prefer to perceive information. Communication and instruction begin with the processing of information that is presented. Understanding sensing and intuitive differences can therefore be critical to improving communication between adults and children and improving the quality of instruction.

Adults can help children appreciate their gifts and recognize their needs.

Adults can help children understand why they find some activities and subjects in school more difficult than others. Adults can help sensing children value their gift for detail and understand that they may have to make an extra effort to determine an activity's theme or main idea. Adults can help intuitive children value their gift for recognizing broad themes and global ideas and teach them to interpret specific messages and recall specific details.

School Applications

One strategy that can help children perform well in school is called *chunking*. With this technique, the adult who is helping the child study for a test can ask the child to look at a page in the book and then identify one main idea on the page and create a topic sentence that describes what is being discussed. This technique is especially helpful with science and social studies materials. The child can then take the topic sentence and add three facts about the topic to it. Visual cues can also help increase memory. Children can imagine words and pictures hanging on to the topic. The topic sentence can then be used to hang the specific pieces of information. For example, if the class is studying wind currents, the topic could be a kite and the related facts could be bows on the kite's tail. If the class is studying volcanoes, the base of the volcano could be the topic theme and the rock, lava, and smoke could be the details. Any item used to aide a child's memory should be one the child is already familiar with. If the child knows nothing about volcanoes, for example, then the volcano image would not be a good choice. Determining the main idea is easier for intuitive students. Chunking is a method for recalling details that can help intuitive students use their gift for patterns and relationships to form images that will enable them to recall specific information.

Review the chapter contents before teaching the material.

School Applications

If the class is going to begin new material, it helps to give students an overview of material in advance. Teachers can walk through a chapter by looking at pictures, noting specific titles, and identifying learning expectations. For example, if the class will be studying a particular Native American culture, the teacher might begin an overview discussion of the material by saying, "This week we will examine the history and culture of the Pueblos. Looking at the picture at the beginning of the chapter, we can see that we will be exploring the types of homes common to this tribe. On the next page, we can see that we will be examining the artistic contributions of the tribe, and on the following page, notice that we will be studying the tribe as it exists today. By the end of this week you should be able to identify how the tribe fed its people, the artistic contributions of the tribe, and the daily life of the tribe members 100 years ago as well as today." By identifying what is expected of them, the teacher makes the children better aware of what information to attend to and enables them to highlight the relevant information as they read the chapter.

The teacher, in this example, can also help students identify the less relevant material in the text. For example, the teacher might say, "Students, on page 15, there is an interesting account of how the tribe used berries and seeds to create dyes. The process is explained in detail. You should read the section, but I will not expect you to describe how the dyes were made." Once this review process is completed, the chapter can then be read. This activity may take only fifteen minutes, but can help intuitive students grasp the total picture to be studied and define for sensing students which details must be learned and which are provided primarily for enrichment. Previewing the materials before the class begins studying them honors type differences and is an activity that can be easily implemented.

Intuitive adults can inadvertently send the wrong message to sensing children.

Home Applications

Young extraverted sensing children will want to share a lot of information with the people around them. Intuitive adults may find it difficult to listen to so many details because of their natural tendency to look for the main idea in a conversation. They may say things like, "Get to the point" or "What is your point?" The young sensing child may have no particular point. The child may simply be sharing all the details of an experience.

Take the experience of a bike ride, for example. A sensing child might describe the experience by saying, "I was riding my bike down Fifth Street when I saw these two dogs. They were big, and I thought they were going to run after me but they didn't. Then I went past the Clark's house and they were painting it blue. When I got to the corner, there was a big pile of dirt on the road and I was going pretty fast so I put on my brakes and slid. I kept sliding around in circles until I skidded into the ground. I wasn't hurt, so I got back up and rode until I got to Mindy's and I told her what happened, and then she helped me clean up so we could play inside." This account is rich with details, but they lead to no specific conclusion. An intuitive child describing the same experience might say, "I rode my bike to Mindy's and fell down on the way." The main idea is present, but the details are noticeably absent.

When intuitive adults impatiently press a child to "get to the point," they send the subtle message that they don't value all of the details the child has to share. To the intuitive adult, the child would better express ideas if they were succinct and to the point. If the intuitive adult does not have the time to listen to the sensing child's wealth of details, it is better to inform the child of this at the onset by saying something along the lines of, "I want to hear as much as I can for five minutes, but then I have to take your sister to soccer practice."

Asking children to rephrase ideas can help raise their level of comprehension.

School Applications

To help children who tend to skip details with schoolwork, adults can ask children to restate the main concept using new words. This works especially well for following directions. Students should be able to state the task directions using their own words. If the directions are accurate, then the intuitive mental leap was effective and the child can begin working. If the student's interpretation of the directions is incorrect, the adult can ask the child to read the directions silently or aloud to determine how the directions differed from the student's original interpretation.

Home Applications

Sometimes parents give their children oral directions and then ask them to repeat the directions to ensure that they understand. Many children can repeat something immediately after hearing it without ever entering the information into their long-term memory. Later, when they are unable to remember the directions, it appears to be the result of irresponsibility. Asking children to rephrase directions using new words can be an effective strategy for helping them increase their comprehension of a task. It's not possible for a person to rephrase the meaning of something without processing at least some of the information. If a child is able to rephrase a set of directions, at least the adult knows that the child understands the task.

Facilitative questioning can encourage children to solve their own problems.

Home and School Applications

Parents and teachers make another mistake when they provide children with suggestions for school projects. Some parents dread the yearly science fair because it means they will have to be more involved with the project than the child. The child comes to the adult and asks, "What can I do for a science project?" The adult answers, "What are you interested in?" The child responds by saying, "I don't know. Anything. Something easy." Then the adult offers a litany of choices —"Do you want to do something with bugs or flowers? How about mold?" The results of such specific suggestions commonly goes in one of two directions—either the child takes the idea and it doesn't work well (in which case the child may take no responsibility for the project's failure) or the child keeps returning to the adult for help. If the project is to grow bread mold, the questions might include, "How long do I have to leave it?", "How can I keep it moldy until the fair?", "Why does it get moldy?", and "Does it matter which bread I use?". In the end, the adult has invested as much time into the project as the child.

But this cycle can be avoided. When the child comes to the adult to ask for suggestions, the adult can follow a procedure called *facilitative questioning* instead of offering specific ideas.

The kinds of questions adults ask facilitate helping children reach their own conclusions. This procedure can work in any situation that requires problem solving. Framing a series of questions that pose a forced choice selection between two options enables adults to facilitate children to solve the problem themselves.

Suppose students are asked to complete an art project and the child then comes to the adult and asks, "What can I do?" The adult can then ask a series of questions that present the child with a forced choice, such as "Do you want to make a painting or a drawing?", "Do you want to make something realistic or abstract?", "Do you want it to be contemporary or historical?", and "Do you want a two-dimensional or a three-dimensional product?". After several questions are answered, the adult can review the child's responses: "You want to make a three-dimensional product that is realistic and depicts something of historical significance. Do you have any ideas yet?" If the child says no, then the adult can continue with questions like, "Do you want American historical significance or world historical significance?" or "Do you want your work to represent this century or some other century?" The important point is that the adult shouldn't suggest an idea. Then the final idea, whenever it comes, will belong to the child. The adult also will have taught the child a strategy for forming ideas so that when the child approaches the adult in the future, the adult can ask if the child went through a list of possible questions to help form a choice. Oftentimes people cannot think of an idea, a project, or a solution to a problem because the field of options is so broad that it seems intangible. Narrowing the field of available options can enable children to manipulate and control the elements that will help them form solutions.

When the child's type is not known, differences can still be accommodated.

Home and School Applications

The greatest difficulty people experience with understanding what other people are saying seems to center around differences between sensing and intuition. If adults are unsure of whether the child prefers sensing or intuition, they can use language to accommodate the differences. For example, let's assume that parents want to discuss vacation plans with their children. They could begin the discussion by saying, "We want to tell you about our vacation plans. We can either tell you what places we will visit and then give you more details later (intuition first, then sensing) or we can tell you how we plan to spend each day (sensing first, then intuition). Which do you prefer?" Children may not be able to tell you that they prefer the sensing way, but, given a choice between a sequential set of information and global information, many can identify which information they prefer. To improve communication, adults do not necessarily need to know a child's type preference, but they do need to be aware of some of the primary differences between the ways intuitive children and sensing children prefer to receive information.

Providing directions as they are needed honors differences.

School Applications

Let's assume a class is asked to write an original story. As soon as the teacher gives the first statement identifying the task, many intuitive students will begin mentally brainstorming possible topics. Meanwhile, the teacher has continued to provide directions for the assignment. Because the intuitives were individually brainstorming, they did not process the teacher's directions. These students are likely to later ask the teacher to repeat the information that was already provided. Many teachers become irritated with students who are not attentive while tasks are being explained. More teachers prefer the sensing function to the intuitive function and therefore deliver directions prior to beginning a task because this is how they would prefer to receive the information. A strategy that honors the different way that sensors and intuitives prefer to receive information is to provide directions as they are needed.

Teachers could begin explaining the story assignment by saying, "The assignment is to write an original story. I will provide as many directions as needed to help you structure your work. When you feel you have a sufficient understanding of the directions, you may begin." Intuitive students may stop being attentive after just a few directions are given. After intuitives have ideas, they need to know details such as the assignment's length and deadline. Sensing children prefer to know these details before they begin to brainstorm possibilities. Teachers who offer children the option of receiving directions as they are needed must also offer them the chance to have directions clarified for about 30 minutes after the directions are first given. If the teacher does not want to have to repeat the directions, the teacher can assign one student to answer questions or the teacher can provide written directions that students can refer to for details. The important point is that adequate direction and examples should be provided prior to the assignment for those students who prefer to have directions before they begin working independently; other students should be allowed to begin working independently and then obtain other directional information when they need it. Providing students with directions in a way that they prefer to receive them is a strategy that honors type differences.

Outlining significant points can provide structure for classroom discussions.

School Applications

Intuitive adults enjoy working with variety and can begin discussing textual information in the middle, then return to the beginning, explain something from the ending, and conclude with more information from the middle. Many intuitive children don't have problems following this kind of thought process. Questions from students can divert an intuitive lecturer from his or her original focus. If students express interest in a subtopic, the intuitive teacher may easily devote a fair amount of instructional time to that subject. In the end, the class may have been enriched by a stimulating discussion but never had the scope of the material presented. Because intuitives can leap comfortably from one thought to another, it may be hard for them to appreciate that this kind of thought pattern can be confusing to others. One way to cope with this difference is to provide students with an outline of significant points for a discussion. The outline would identify points of a discussion, including those not discussed in class, and enable students to ask for further clarification of points that were not addressed.

Another helpful strategy was suggested by a student. Teachers are expected to review previous material before they introduce new material. One student, who had a particularly difficult time separating old material from new, asked if the teacher would just make a statement indicating when old material was being reviewed and when new material was being introduced. This student was so busy trying to take thorough notes that she could not attend to the information being presented. Two sentences that the teacher used to identify material eased her stress and enabled her to listen to the review without being concerned with note taking. Before reviewing material, the teacher simply identified the material as "review." Before presenting new material, the teacher said, "This information is new and not yet in your notes." Devoting a short period of time to structuring the material enabled the student to participate more fully in the lesson and discussion.

The language adults use to design tasks can influence the way students respond to them.

School Applications

Teachers can unintentionally limit the way students respond to tasks by the language they use to define them. When teachers use verbs such as describe, name, or define, the verb practically classifies the information they are requesting. Regardless of what the student's preference may be, verbs such as these ask for sensing data. When the teacher uses terms such as brainstorm, explore, web, connect, or create, the task draws on the intuitive skill of using information to form patterns and conclusions. No matter what the child's preference, the task can be defined by the language used. All children will respond in a sensing way to the first set of verbs given above and in an intuitive way to the second set of verbs presented. The difference will be evident in how difficult a task is for a student and in the amount of energy needed to complete it. Intuitive students generally find tasks that ask them to describe, name, or define things more fatiguing, and sensing students are likely to find tasks that ask them to brainstorm, explore, web, connect, or create more fatiguing. Some teachers do not intentionally limit the task to one function over the other, but their choice of language when they provide directions can override their intentions.

Unclear directions can cause confusion.

School Applications

Intuitive teachers can find it difficult to write clear, concise directions. The lack of detail which is so evident to sensors reading the instructions is not evident to the intuitive who designs the directions with the assumption that the meaning is clear. For example, an intuitive teacher gave a class the direction to list the planets in order. The intuitive teacher felt this was a very direct, simple, clear statement. Sensing students challenged the teacher with questions such as, "Do you want them in order from the sun, alphabetical order, order of size, or order of origin?"

Sensing teachers may write clear directions for intuitives, but many intuitive students admit they don't read directions. Instead they use examples to infer the task directions. When the task is open-ended, a sensing teacher can offer so many directions that the intuitive choices are limited.

Summary

A variety of strategies can enhance the learning environment for sensing and intuitive students. Teachers who use type awareness to structure classroom presentations promote instructional effectiveness in the classroom.

- Using mnemonic strategies can help students recall details.

- Previewing material can be helpful to both types for different reasons.

- Sensing children share rich details and adults should recognize this ability.

- Rephrasing directions increases recall better than memorization because a higher level of mental processing is required to reconstruct words than is required to repeat them.

- Facilitative questioning is a strategy that can help increase the problem-solving skills of all children.

- Providing directions as they are needed honors the different learning styles of both sensing and intuitive students.

- Intuitive teachers who provide outlines of significant points are able to clearly identify important points that may not be addressed in class discussions.

- The language used to describe a task can limit the way students respond to it.

■ ■

Chapter 11

Building Positive Relationships With Thinking and Feeling Children

The thinking and feeling functions develop after the perceiving functions of sensing and intuition. It may be difficult to distinguish these functions in young children. The suggestions provided in this chapter may therefore be appropriate for school-age children.

Children with a thinking preference need to be able to answer the question why.

Home and School Applications

Children with a thinking preference ask why they have to do tasks, why something works, and why they have to behave certain ways. These questions are not challenges to authority and adults should answer them. Children with a thinking preference value comments that are clear, logical, and fair.

An established relationship helps children with a feeling preference accept critical feedback.

School Applications

Children with a feeling preference value frequent feedback about their performance. Positive feedback reinforces their behaviors and they can accept negative feedback if they have a positive relationship with the person providing it. People with a feeling preference are not just receptive to positive feedback, but they do need reassurance that the feedback about their shortcomings will not affect the positive relationship they have already established. People who have shared experiences and know each other well are therefore able to provide more direct criticism to these children than less familiar adults. Teachers who know their students are in a better position to provide critical feedback that feeling children can accept.

Active listening is a strategy that helps children process their thinking and affective feelings.

Home Applications

Some adults try to probe to find out what a child is really thinking and they do this by asking the child a lot of questions. Many children, particularly in the older grades, resent being asked a lot of questions and view it as a form of intrusion. A child might state, "I don't want to perform in the concert tonight." An adult with a thinking preference might take the next logical step and ask why. Children cannot always explain themselves and may simply know that they just don't want to perform. When an adult asks for an explanation and the child doesn't produce a reason that is acceptable to the adult, some adults react by saying things like, "If you don't have a good reason for not going, then the discussion is over." A better strategy is for the adult to engage in active listening techniques.

When children make statements, adults should respond in a way that reflects the content of the child's statement rather than just asking questions. It is equally important that they reflect the tone of the child's original statement. Reflection does not amount to simply parroting back the child's exact words but is rather a restatement of the child's words using language that honors the content and the feeling of the child's message.

An adult might respond to the child's original statement about not wanting to perform in the concert by saying, "You don't feel like going to the concert tonight." Some adults familiar with this strategy have learned to use it when they first respond to a child's statements but then quickly revert to old habits with successive responses. These adults follow up their active listening statements by asking the child "Why?" or "Why not?" The why question compels children to develop reasons for their decision, and most children assume that reasons they provide must be acceptable to the adult or else they will be challenged. Since the child may not be able to articulate his or her feelings or since telling the real reason would reveal information the child may not want the adult to know (such as having had a fight with a girlfriend or boyfriend), the child usually responds by saying, "I don't know." These words, perhaps more than any others, seem to irritate parents and teachers. The adult typically responds to the child's statement by asking, "Why don't you know?" or "What do you mean you don't know?" The child might then respond with, "I just don't," and the conversation ends.

A better exchange between the adult and child might resemble the conversation below, which incorporates active listening strategies.

> *Adult*: "You don't feel like going to the concert tonight." (The child should be given as much time as he or she needs to respond. If the adult interrupts the child's thoughts by talking, the adult takes control of the conversation, and the door should be left open for the child to lead the discussion.)
>
> *Child*: "No, I don't."
>
> *Adult*: "You really wish you didn't have to go."
>
> *Child*: "Sometimes I just don't want to have to do everything or go everywhere, or be everything."
>
> *Adult*: "You think that sometimes people get tired of trying to do everything or be everything for others."
>
> *Child*: "That's right. I mean, Sally thinks I should talk with her every day, and if I talk to Jane, she gets mad at me. I should be able to talk to whoever I want and Sally should just chill out."

Adult: "It's upsetting when one friend tells you what to do with your other friends, is that it?"

Child: "Sally told me not to ride with Jane to the concert, but Jane offered me a ride and I told her yes. If Sally sees us riding together, she'll never speak to me again."

Adult: "You seem worried about what Sally will think when she sees you come to the concert with Jane. Is there a solution?"

Child: "I better just call Sally and tell her. Then she can get mad at me on the phone instead of in front of everyone. I'll offer to pick her up, too, if she wants, but I doubt she will. Sometimes having two best friends can be a real pain."

If adults allow children more time to talk and take on the role of listener instead of advice-giver, it can be a real tool for building positive adult-child relationships. Without the use of active listening strategies to help guide the adult's language, some adults advise their children "not to worry," since Sally is the one who is causing the problem, or they share that when they were the child's age, they had a best friend in school who acted similarly. The conversation becomes a vehicle for the adult to share stories about the past rather than a focus on the present needs of the child.

Most advice such as this is ignored. The message the adult sends to the child is, "Adults don't listen or understand," and the child is less likely to share future problems. The worst comment an adult can make to a child who is revealing his or her feelings is, "I know just how you feel." This statement closes the door to the child's sharing and assumes that the way the adult experienced past situations replicates the way the child is currently experiencing a particular situation. Understanding type differences can highlight the fact that not all individuals experience similar situations in similar ways. Active listening strategies can help separate underlying problems from initial statements.

Language that comes naturally to many people with a feeling preference is difficult for people with a thinking preference to produce. They agree that the words used in active listening seem appropriate but state that they would never think of those words in the midst of a conversation. If language that expresses sensitivity to the needs of other people doesn't come naturally, then the words can be learned. Practice will improve these kinds of language skills over time. People with a thinking preference can practice using active listening skills and become adept at honoring the affective needs of children whose preferences may not be clearly established.

Summarizing what other people have said allows misperceptions to be clarified.

Home Applications

Those with a thinking preference might also investigate how other people interpret their language. Many are shocked to learn that what they intended as descriptive feedback was interpreted as a personal attack. For example, a father with a thinking preference asked his preteen daughter, "Do you really like your hair that way?" The child was asked to restate what her father had just said to her and she responded, "Dad says I'm ugly." The father argued that that was not what he said, but the child didn't listen. As far as the father was concerned, his comment was restricted to the child's hair and reflected his preference for certain hairstyles. To him, it only amounted to one person's opinion. The child inferred a deeper meaning. This seems to be a common source of conflict between adults with a thinking preference and children with a feeling preference. Unless the father had asked his daughter to restate his comment, he would never have known that his words were misinterpreted. Many thinkers believe that they send a clear message when a completely different one is actually received. The strategy for resolving this potential source of conflict is to ask the receiver to restate the original statement. When a message with possible emotional overtones has been sent, the receiver can be asked to restate what they think was said. If the message was sent and received correctly, the issues are clear. If not, the sender can clarify the message before the receiver internalizes the inferred meaning.

Some children with a feeling preference need to be taught how to evaluate their work.

Some people with a feeling preference have admitted that their need to please others can interfere with their development of the ability to form independent opinions. Some with a feeling preference admit to spending more time trying to figure out what the other person wants them to say than they do actually deciding how they feel about a topic. Young children seem especially susceptible to changing their opinions to match an adult's in order to gain acceptance. The adult may not be sending the message that the child should agree with the adult's opinion and may even be encouraging the child to form an independent opinion, but simply telling the child with a feeling preference not to be influenced by the opinion of others is inadequate. The child needs to be taught a strategy for forming independent, detached opinions. For example, the child could be taught to critically analyze his or her work efforts by following some of the systematic approaches offered below.

School Applications

Let's assume a child with a feeling preference just drew a picture in an art class. The child then takes the drawing to the teacher and asks, "Did I do a good job?" The teacher has a choice of giving feedback or asking the child to evaluate the quality of the work first. If the teacher wants the child to form independent judgments, the teacher might respond by saying, "What do you think?" The child might respond, "I don't know," and the teacher again has the choice of providing feedback or encouraging the child to form an independent, personal evaluation. To encourage this kind of independence, the teacher could say, "I'm going to write what I think is good or not good about your picture, and you can write what you think is good or not good about it. Then we can compare our lists." Children who depend on the opinion of others will find this task extremely difficult and will in all likelihood resist it initially. But giving the child the opportunity to evaluate the work, even if the analysis is never completed, confirms that the child's opinion of the work is equally valuable to the adult's opinion.

Another procedure provides children with step-by-step instructions that enables them to become detached from their work and produce an objective analysis. Children can be taught the following steps as one possible way of evaluating their work before they seek the opinion of others. In the case of the example with the drawing, the following steps could be used. Children should:

- Pretend someone else drew the picture
- Assume they do not know the person who drew the picture and that they will not meet the person
- Look at the design and ask themselves if it is attractive, original, and valuable
- Name two positive things about the work and write them down
- Name one aspect of the drawing that might be improved, if any, and write it down
- Form an overall conclusion about the merits of the work by comparing it to drawings done by other students
- Sign the drawing and their evaluation to claim ownership of the strengths and limitations of the drawing as well as to claim ownership of their evaluation of the piece

Children who have strong visual skills can sometimes try a similar procedure that takes only a minute. Let's assume a child has asked for the teacher's opinion about a drawing and, when the teacher asks for the child's opinion, the response is, "I don't know." The teacher might then draw a line with a tick mark at the beginning and the end. The teacher could say, "The mark on the left is for the very worst drawing ever produced by any child at any time in the world, and the mark on the right is for the very best work ever produced by any child at any time in the world. Draw a mark somewhere on the line to show how you think your work compares." After the child draws a mark, the teacher can then ask the child to identify one positive characteristic of the work that warranted the placement on the scale and one characteristic of the work the child feels could stand improvement. This enables the child to form not only a global impression of the work's value but also at least one specific strength and one area where the work could be improved. The analysis only takes a moment or two but helps to develop the thinking skills of children with a feeling preference.

Children with thinking and feeling preferences hear praise differently.

Home and School Applications

Children with a thinking preference tend to value praise that recognizes their competence, whereas children with a feeling preference tend to value praise that recognizes their worth and their contributions. Telling a thinking child, "You were wonderful!" would often amount to inadequate praise. These children want specific, credible praise that tells them why their work or behavior is being recognized. Vague praise raises concerns about what the sender really intended. Praise for both thinking and feeling types must be sincere. Examples of praise that would be acceptable for children with a thinking preference might include:

- "That was intelligent"
- "These are good ideas"
- "You're going above and beyond"
- "Brilliantly done"
- "You're meeting job expectations"

Behaviors that would be accepted as praise by thinking students might include:

- Praise from teachers and other adults, which is generally valued more than praise from peers
- Teachers and other adults using their ideas
- Being given another equally challenging job because of their previous successes with similar tasks

- Teachers and other adults using their ideas and giving them credit for them

Examples of praise that would be acceptable for children with a feeling preference might include:

- "Great job, Joe" (Using the child's name is important)
- "Wow!" "Super!"
- "Your project was wonderful"
- "I can tell you put a lot of thought and effort into your project"
- "I appreciate the effort and organization you put into your work"
- "I like the way you did that"

Behaviors that would be accepted as praise by feeling students might include:

- A pat on the back
- A handshake
- A smile
- Stickers
- Personal comments on work
- Addressing the person by name
- Personal notes in classes
- Direct eye contact
- A hug
- Positive gestures such as a thumbs up or a high five

Not all of these examples will work in all instances. For example, some children with a feeling preference would find a hug offensive and wonder if there were issues of control behind the gesture. Smiley faces on children's papers may not be used because the teacher with a thinking preference can't identify with the value of the symbol. In general, those with a feeling preference prefer that praise be personalized, and those with a thinking preference seem to value praise that recognizes achievement and is offered by an authority figure. Being aware that different types perceive praise differently is a step toward improving adult-child relationships.

Providing a choice of test questions permits different types to demonstrate their learning.

School Applications

The design and language of test questions was discussed earlier. Providing children with some choices when they answer test questions is included in this chapter because it seems to honor the need for fairness in students. Tests are samples of student learning. If students do not all learn things the same way but all complete the school year with the same amount of accurate information, have they all learned equally? Can tests be designed to measure differences in student learning style preferences while still measuring equal achievement? One strategy that can help meet both needs is to give students some choice in how they answer test questions. If a history test covers five chapters, for example, the test could be constructed so that thirteen questions are devoted to addressing the content in each chapter. Students could then be given the option of choosing ten out of the possible thirteen questions to answer for each chapter. Each question would be worth two points and grading would not be difficult. This allows the teacher to assess each student's knowledge of each chapter while still allowing students some choice in how they answer test questions. Many students have reported that they believe this system is more fair than requiring them to anticipate exactly which questions will be on the test.

Students have also suggested that teachers allow them to preview tests that the teacher gave previously before they take the first exam that semester. Students get a flavor for the teacher's question design, format, and assessment style. This exposure to test format affects the way students study and can help some students structure their study habits more effectively.

Summary

Building positive relationships with thinking and feeling children requires an understanding of how each type perceives praise, accepts feedback, and expresses ideas. Strategies specific for each type honor the developing personality of the child.

- Children with a feeling preference are better able to accept critical feedback from people they have established positive relationships with.

- Active listening is a strategy that can help students process their thinking and affective feelings.

- Skills not natural to a type can be learned.

- Verifying that the message received accurately reflects the message sent is a strategy that can improve communication between people with thinking and feeling preferences.

- Children with a feeling preference can be taught skills that enable them to detach themselves from their work and form objective self-evaluations.

- Praise should always be genuine but can be interpreted differently by children with thinking and feeling preferences.

- Providing students with a choice of test questions allows them to accurately demonstrate what they have learned without requiring every student to answer the same questions.

CHAPTER 12

Building Positive Relationships With Judging and Perceiving Children

The judging and perceiving attitudes seem to affect patterns of living together more than they influence patterns of communication or information processing. Judging and perceiving differences can bring about conflict in the classroom and home environment surrounding such issues as homework, rule compliance, closure needs, and flexibility. These differences can be evident even in young children and can strain the tolerance of everyone involved. Strategies to better understand and cope with differences between judging and perceiving children can help promote healthier adult-child relationships.

Forward planning helps children with judging preferences, and backward planning helps children with perceiving preferences.

Home Applications

Many young perceiving students have a difficult time meeting deadlines. Adults with the same preference have learned to "beat the clock" and tend to complete work exactly when it is due and not much sooner. Young children cannot rely on their experience, so they will often misjudge how long a task will take to complete. Young perceiving children typically believe they can complete a six-week project the night before it is due. When this occurs, the family with a judging preference can become involved in a big argument about responsibility and the importance of beginning an assignment immediately after it is given. The entire household can then become stressed. In contrast, families with a perceiving preference sometimes enjoy the thrill of the last-minute rush to complete work and can become energized helping the child to make adjustments when materials are found to be unavailable or when ideas must be substituted because of time constraints.

Perceiving children need help learning to schedule their time working backward from a deadline to determine the last possible minute they can begin the project and still expect to complete it on time. This method of scheduling isn't a form of procrastination. Perceiving children tend to think better with the pressure of a looming deadline, and a clear deadline often stimulates them to do their best. Even if the perceiving child begins working on the task when it is assigned, the child's best work may not materialize until the deadline nears.

Perceiving children like to think about and plan their work on projects over longer periods. Once they begin to actually work on a project they have already eliminated their options for the project. Since perceivers love to keep all their options open as long as they possibly can, it makes sense that they would not actually begin work on a project until the last possible moment.

The problem that young perceiving children encounter is that they inaccurately judge how long it will take them to complete projects. Adults can facilitate the development of this skill in children by helping them consider all the possible variables that might interfere with the project's completion. Adults should let children identify the latest possible time they can begin a project. If the project is due on Monday, for example, some perceiving children will believe they can start working on it Sunday night. Adults can then help children gain a more realistic picture of timeline limitations. For instance, let's assume a child states that she can begin a history project Sunday night. The adult might then ask, "Didn't you have to do some library research?" Now the child concedes work must begin Saturday morning. The adult can then remind the child of other considerations: "Don't you have a soccer game on Saturday?" The child then realizes that she must begin working on the project on Friday. And the adult can then remind the child of still other considerations: "Isn't your grandmother coming to visit on Friday night and isn't your family planning to go out to dinner after she arrives?" The realization that the project should be started on Thursday when Thursday seems light years away from Monday morning is difficult for the child to accept. By scheduling backward from the project's deadline and helping the child consider all the possible intervening variables, the adult provides the child with a strategy that can be used for future project planning.

Deadlines don't enhance the abilities of the student with a judging preference. In the case of these students, an approaching deadline adds stress and if the deadline begins to close in and the project is not completed, the child's thinking begins to fragment and their work becomes less effective. Teaching these children to schedule backward from a deadline would not honor their natural preference to begin working on assignments as soon as possible to bring closure to the task. These children need help designing a schedule that works forward from the date the task is assigned to the deadline. Judgers seem to have a better sense of time and how long it will take them to complete projects. Judging children also need to consider extraneous intervening variables, but the timeline itself will help determine whether the task can be accomplished at a reasonable rate. The timeline can also provide a helpful reference when these children receive other assignments that might conflict with the schedule of this or other existing tasks.

Assigning deadlines helps both types for different reasons.

Home Applications

Children with a judging preference need deadlines to help them determine how much work they need to do and whether they can commit to new obligations with their current schedule. Those with a perceiving preference need deadlines to help initiate a task. One father with a judging preference had a difficult time getting his daughter, who had a perceiving preference, to prepare for bedtime. He was a single parent and needed her cooperation. Bedtime rituals began early but lasted several hours while the child played in the tub, played as she was dressed in her bedtime clothes, and then played with whatever toys or things came within her view. The father tried nagging and using frequent prompts, such as "Hurry up" and "Finish what you're doing," but none were successful. The father finally used type awareness to help remedy the situation and set a bedtime deadline.

The girl loved to have her father read her a story before she went to bed. The father set a rule that story time began at 8 P.M. sharp. He would begin reading the bedtime story whether or not his daughter was in her bed at that time. Initially, only a few stuffed animals heard the tales, but it didn't take long before the child began to pace her play, bath time, and related bedtime activities so that she could be in bed when her father began to read the evening's story. There was no need for the father to nag and remind his daughter about her bedtime, since the deadline took their place. Both the father and daughter were better able to enjoy each other.

The judging child can become stressed when deadlines are spontaneously imposed by parents. If no one paid attention to how long it took the child to get ready in the morning and suddenly the child is expected to take a bath, brush his or her teeth, and get ready for school in ten minutes, it can be stressful. These children don't want to be rushed and appreciate when people respect their need to have enough time to do things.

Games rather than rules can help perceiving children get organized.

Home Applications

It might be helpful for young perceiving children to have designated places to keep all of their things. One parent had a very young perceiving child who had severe organizational problems. His solution was to tape pictures of keys, books, glasses, and pencils to the top of the child's dresser. The child was then expected to place the real items on top of the matching pictures each day when she returned home from school. If the items were not placed correctly by the child's bedtime, the child was expected to find the items so that the frantic searching game would not have to be played out in the morning. Simply telling perceiving children to organize their materials is not effective. Even if the materials were organized for them (and many parents do this), materials would once again become out of order within a few weeks.

Other perceiving children have found it helpful to mentally walk through each of their classes before they leave for school in the morning. As they visualize themselves in each of their classes, they mentally note whatever books, homework, and supplies they will need. Lunch and returning home are both part of the day so that lunch money and house keys are part of the memory chain. Children may need help using this strategy. Parents can help by mentally walking through the day with the child with the understanding that this strategy will be practiced independently once the child gets older.

Adult lectures are only effective when children listen to them.

Home Applications

Children with a judging preference tend to lead their lives in terms of shoulds and oughts. Rules and expectations need to be made clear to these children so that they know what to do. Parents with a judging preference tend to advise and lecture their children frequently. One cartoon appropriately captured how some children respond to such an approach with a caption that read, "Instead of a long boring lecture, couldn't you give me a snappy one-liner?" In reality, most children do not listen to their parent's full lectures. One rule that has helped some families limit the amount of lecturing allows the person who is being lectured to stop the person giving the lecture at any time by restating the point of the lecture. If the person accurately restates the point of the lecture, then the lecturer has to stop. Children love having this kind of control, but while parents can be sure that their messages were heard, they may find it frustrating that their well-planned lectures will not be heard by anyone.

An awareness of type differences can help with gift buying.

Home Applications

Around the holidays, an incredible amount of television advertising entices children to want everything. Parents with a judging preference probe to find out what their children want and many purchase as much as they can well in advance so they can be sure to get what their children want. But then the tendencies of perceiving children come into the picture. Within a week, these children may change their minds and no longer want what they originally asked for. Within a few days, they might change their minds again. Parents with a judging preference can't tell young children that everything they asked for has been purchased and is already hidden in a closet, so they might typically respond by saying, "You want everything you see. You're so selfish. Can't you make up your mind?" The parents' frustration becomes misdirected, and the children do not understand what they did wrong. They don't understand why their parents are upset.

One possible solution is to tell perceiving children to be careful about the way they tell a parent what they want. Instead of stating their choice by saying , "I want a skateboard," they would be better off saying, "I think I might want a skateboard, but I'm not sure yet." Perceivers like to keep their options open until the very last minute, and for children the last minute is often the day they are to receive the gift. When children phrase their selections with the qualification that it may not be their final choice, parents clearly understand that the children have not made a decision.

To be fair to judging parents, perceiving children should be given a calendar and told that they have to make up their minds by a certain date. Children must then make their decisions by the deadline and not be allowed to change after that time. If they see something later that they would prefer, they should be told that it will have to be put aside until the next occasion for gift-giving. Children find this approach acceptable. The strategy honors the perceiving child's need to delay decisions until the deadline, yet respects the parent's need to buy gifts well enough in advance of an event. Type allows families to work toward solutions that honor both the adult and the child's preferences, and this always leads to better adult-child relationships.

Advising judging and perceiving children of impending closure can increase cooperation.

Home and School Applications

It is important to warn judging and perceiving childrens in advance that the time allowed for a task is almost up. Those with a judging preference need to bring closure to the task. Perhaps students have finished a class assignment and are talking about what they might do after school. They will still need time to finish their conversation and bring closure to their thoughts. Perceivers need advance warning so that they can be sure to finish the assigned task. Teachers need only say, "Two more minutes. Finish what you can." Parents can use this same closure warning for time allowed for playing outside, and teachers can use this strategy to announce the end of recess. Providing a signal to bring closure to an event or activity respects the needs of children with both judging and perceiving preferences.

Having supplies on hand honors both types for different reasons.

School Applications

A group of teachers being trained in type concepts was told a story about a child with a perceiving preference. The child's parent knew that sometime during the course of the school year, the child would be watching television and ask, "Do we have any poster board? I have a project due tomorrow and I need some."

Because the parent did not want to go out in the middle of the week to purchase poster board, the materials were purchased at the beginning of the school year and kept on hand for emergencies. Teachers responded to the story with negative comments, stating that they felt the parent's approach did not teach the child responsibility and allowed the student to perpetuate bad habits.

Another group of teachers was told a similar story about a child with a judging preference. The child's parent knew that sometime during the course of the school year, the child would come home and say, "Do we have any poster board? I have a big project due and I need to get started right away." The parent asked, "When is it due?" And the child said, "Not for a week, but I need to get started right away. It's a big part of our grade." Because the parent did not want to go to the store in the middle of the week to purchase poster board, the materials were purchased at the beginning of the school year and kept on hand for emergencies. This time, the teachers supported the parent's approach and felt it was an appropriate strategy to use. Data support that more teachers prefer judging than perceiving. More teachers were therefore able to identify with the judging child's need to begin a project immediately after it was assigned, but fewer were able to identify with the perceiving child's need to delay work on a project until the deadline became imminent. Understanding such type differences can increase an appreciation of different learning styles.

Advice and assistance that meet a child's needs will be most helpful.

Home Applications

Children with a judging preference must complete work before they can rest. This means that some older children will be up quite late at night completing their assignments. A parent who sees the child working late and tells the child to "go to bed" or "get up early to finish" doesn't offer advice that respects the child's learning style. It would be more helpful if the parent said,

"Can I make you a cup of hot chocolate or put your books in a pile or get you a pillow to sit on?" Helping these children become comfortable respects their need to complete the work before going to bed and demonstrates an empathy for the stress they may be experiencing at that moment. If possible, parents might offer to assume some of the children's household chores to allow enough time for judging children to begin working on their homework earlier. Telling these children to "relax" ignores their natural style.

Summary

Strategies to enhance the natural gifts of the judging and perceiving child are necessary during the developmental years. These are especially important when a parent's or teacher's type differs from the child's.

- Forward planning helps judging children, and backward planning helps perceiving children.
- Assigning deadlines helps both types for different reasons.
- Games rather than rules can help perceiving children become more organized.
- When the child being lectured can demonstrate an understanding of the parent's message, then the lecture should end.
- Type can be used to help families cope with gift buying.
- Giving an advance warning that an activity is about to end allows both types to conclude tasks and increases cooperation.
- Having supplies available honors both types for different reasons.
- Parental advice and assistance should match a child's type needs.

Chapter 13

■ ■

Suggestions for Improving Relationships With Children of All Types

Some of the suggestions for improving adult-child relationships do not specifically address different preferences but help encourage an awareness of different issues that will increase the understanding that adults and children have of each other. This chapter will address issues that relate to all sixteen personality types.

It's best to honor the type of the person who has the greater emotional need.

Should a tired mother be expected to listen to her extraverted child tell her all about his day immediately after she returns home from work, or should the child be taught to wait to tell his story and respect his mother's need for quiet time? A good rule might be to accommodate the type needs of the person who has the greater emotional need unless the child is of preschool age. Very young children will find it difficult to adjust to the needs of adults, but older children can accommodate the needs of others.

If the mother finds it difficult to listen to her son and needs some quiet time, she can go to another room and tell her child that sharing time will be after dinner, or some other set time. Children can respond to time determined by specific events better than abstract times such as "in a while" or "in thirty minutes." In the example described, it is the mother who has the greater emotional need. If the child is feeling frustrated or abandoned, then the parent should delay the need for quiet time and listen to what the child has to share. If the child's stories go on incessantly, the parent can set a timer for five minutes and tell the child that there are five minutes for sharing now and that after mother rests, there will be more time for sharing. Most children can adjust to this kind of request.

When children are under stress they rely most on their natural preferences.

Each person has the ability to use all of the functions and attitudes. Children appear to experiment with and explore the use of their less-preferred functions until they experience stress. In times of stress, children seem to select activities that respect their natural preferences. Coping with stress requires energy, and there is no mental energy available for working on projects that overextend children's processing abilities. When life is more relaxed, sensing children might select an intuitive activity or the intuitive child might select a sensing activity. During times of stress, however, sensing children seem to select sensing projects and intuitive children tend to select intuitive projects. Because the personality types of children are still developing, they should be given a choice of learning activities that honor the four functions (sensing, intuition, thinking, and feeling) whenever possible.

Understanding type preferences can help explain people's motives.

Not all statements mean exactly what they first appear to mean. If a child says, "I don't want to go on that field trip," there might be many reasons for this statement. A child with a feeling preference might not want to go on the trip because of an argument with a friend, who is also planning to go on the trip. A child with a thinking preference might not want to go on the trip because the description of the place doesn't sound interesting. A child with a judging preference might not want to go on the trip because the teacher gave a new assignment to the class and going on the field trip would mean that there might not be sufficient time to complete the assignment. A child with a perceiving preference might not want to go on the trip because the same field trip has been scheduled two years running and it's getting boring. It's important for adults to become accustomed to not reacting to the first statements that children make and try to discover the underlying motives behind the comments or behaviors. Suggestions for ways children can resolve problems are more effective if they match children's true needs as well as the needs they express.

Type should never be an excuse for failing to meet an expectation.

Type should never be allowed as an excuse for not meeting an academic or family expectation. If a child is expected to be home at 6 P.M., then the child should be home at 6 P.M. regardless of the child's type. Type awareness can help adults understand that the perceiving child will have more difficulty keeping track of the time than the judging child. Some perceiving children have found that wearing a watch with an alarm helps them to get home on time. By that same token, adults should not set expectations that children cannot meet. Expecting a child with a perceiving preference to naturally adopt judging characteristics denies the inherent differences between the two types. Adults should keep in mind that perceivers can learn to meet expectations in perceiving ways and judgers can learn to meet expectations in judging ways.

Type does not predict behaviors.

Many adults wonder if knowing a child's type will enable them to anticipate what the child will do or say in any situation. Children often ask the same question. Children wonder if adults who know their type can make them do things they don't want to. Both concerns address the issue of control. Can someone use an awareness of type to control the behavior of other people?

An awareness of type only provides insight into what a person might prefer to do in a given situation. Each person has free will and the ability to use all of the different attitudes and functions. Choosing the function or attitude that matches situational needs is a matter of individual choice. Introverts can, for example, act extraverted, sensors can use intuition, and so on. Part of development is helping children recognize situational demands and identify how to use personality strengths to meet the needs of particular situations. There may be other factors not related to type preference that influence a child's behavioral response in a specific situation. Type won't explain everything.

Rewarding learning rather than task mastery can be effective with all types.

Many adults encounter problems when they use reward charts to reward children for performing expected skills. For instance, if a child is rewarded by having a star sticker placed on a chart every day that they make the bed, then at what point does the program cease? If the adult stops putting stickers on the chart, does the child then no longer feel incentive and therefore stop making the bed? Additionally, if the adult places stickers on a chart to recognize when a seven-year-old makes the bed each day, should the same be done for a nine-year-old who does the same task? The problem with rewarding specific behaviors is that the focus is placed on the activity and not on the learning period. Is making a bed equally difficult for a younger and older child? If it isn't, then rewarding the bed-making behavior is not fair. Parents can avoid this issue if they make reward charts that recognize when children learn new skills. Then children can be treated equally and a similar star chart can be used. Each child would have a separate skill to learn. The star sticker would be given whenever children made progress with their particular skills. Once children master a particular skill, parents can explain that the mastered skill, such as long division, is no longer considered a new skill. Once children learn new skills, they can just be expected to continue doing them. So, if the child wants to continue using the reward chart, the child and the parent can decide what new skills the child needs to practice. It is fair to reward children identically when they learn new skills. It is not fair to reward children identically for performing the same tasks.

Some adults who have particular preferences will find it difficult or even frustrating to use reward charts. They forget to chart children's progress or are unable to consistently mark progress on a daily basis or only remember to chart a child's progress when it becomes apparent that problems are surfacing. Not all adults are comfortable using reward charts and not all adults should use them. If this is a strategy that does not meet the needs of both the adult and the child, its effectiveness will be limited. Adults who recognize their gifts and limitations as well as the gifts and limitations of the children they have relationships with are able to design effective intervention programs. Every activity should meet the type needs of both the adult and the child.

Ethical guidelines for using type instruments with children should be followed.

Every adult taking a personality inventory has the right to receive feedback about the results and disagree with them. Children should have the same right. The results of any instrument that a child completes should be given directly to the child so that he or she has the opportunity to ask questions. The child's parent or teacher can be part of the feedback session, but the adult involved should not receive any feedback about the child that the child does not also receive.

Children benefit when they understand their growth and development. Type development is a part of this process, so helping children become aware of type differences is a positive activity. Adults should not, however, insist that a child complete an assessment instrument. Children's participation in determining their type preferences should be voluntary. Assessment instruments are only tools that help individuals determine type preferences.

Assessment instruments can provide children with opportunities to express their inner feelings and thoughts. Adults may at times hypothesize a child's type preferences. One possible danger inherent in projecting a type onto a child is that the adult will react to the child as if the assessment is the child's actual preference. Only individuals can identify their true preferences. Allowing children to use an assessment instrument to identify their type preferences respects their right to confirm or deny the results.

The meaning of type is personal.

Scientific inquiry can verify the way blood travels through the body. We can identify this as a fact. Scientific inquiry can only lend support to theories of personality development. Personality is not a concrete entity but is rather an inferred entity that is based on an individual's thought and behavior properties. Psychological type is one way of defining individual personality. Research with adults supports the theory that attitudes and functions develop over time and that personality types describe real and valid differences in the way people perceive information and communicate and interact with others. Most of the knowledge available about children and type development is based on observations of children's behaviors. There is no definitive "proof" that type descriptions are accurate. However, the descriptions of type do seem to define the behaviors of children well. Children who have been taught type concepts react with the same sense of completeness that adults experience when the value of their type preference is validated. Children have identified with type profiles and have used the information contained in them to redirect their behaviors. If children did not find meaning in type concepts, it is unlikely that they would change their behaviors. Children have been known to teach their friends about type because they found it to be a clear and helpful way to interpret the behaviors of their peers and the adults in their lives.

Bridges build better relationships between adults and children.

Bridging by attitude and bridging by action are steps to build positive connections between adults and children. For example, viewing an extraverted child's talking as a need to share information about the world is quite different from viewing the talking as uncontrollable noise. Attitude inspires reactions. If a child's behavior is acceptable, it is treated differently than a behavior that is considered unacceptable. Understanding type can allow adults to appreciate the qualities of all types, to define acceptable behaviors for the different types, and to build bridges with positive attitudes.

When an adult does something specifically to address the special uniqueness of a child, the adult is building a connection with actions. For example, parents of sensing children who explain information in ways that are receptive to sensors and parents of judging children who help their children plan ahead for a family vacation are responding with actions that honor their children's individuality. These actions build positive bridges that help improve adult-child relationships.

Type is only one aspect of individual development.

The total child, including all aspects of development, should be considered as well as the environment surrounding the child. Defining differences can simplify complex behaviors and seem to diminish individual complexity.

Thus, an understanding of types helps describe people's behaviors, offers a framework for appreciating differences, and increases an awareness of the developmental needs of children. As rich as this tool is in explaining behavior, humans are still complex. Descriptions are only examples and no person is bound to act according to preferences. Elements in the environment and in the child's unconscious can affect the choice of behavior in any situation. Although the nature of individuals is complex, understanding parts of personality development can open more windows for improving relationships. We may, of course, choose to ignore these differences until type differences are verified by research, but observations and experience confirm the validity of the differences. The value of recognizing the template of type differences can only improve relationships between adults and children.

Summary

Some strategies apply to all types. These strategies help build relationships and protect the developing nature of the child.

- Honor the type of the individual who has the greater emotional need unless the child is of preschool age.
- Stress reduces an individual's ability to be flexible.
- It is important to consider the motive behind people's actions.
- Type should never be used as an excuse for failing to meet an expectation.
- Type does not predict behaviors.
- Rewarding learning rather than mastery of specific tasks can be used with all types.
- An adult who has a relationship with a child should not be given the child's type results unless the child also receives them.
- Instruments to measure type are tools and should be taken voluntarily.
- Bridging differences with attitude and by actions builds better relationships between adults and children.
- While type is only one aspect of individual development, an awareness of type can improve adult-child relationships.

References and Resources

Hirsh, S., and J. Kummerow. *Lifetypes*. NY: Warner Books, 1989. This book describes the basic differences that exist in human beings. It uses excellent examples and describes how these differences can influence various aspects of our lives.

Jung, C. G. *Psychological Types*. A 1971 revision by R. F. C. Hull of the translation by H. G. Baynes. Princeton, NJ: Princeton University Press. This book contains a general description of the psychological types and definitions of Jung's principal psychological concepts. The book relates type to history, literature, and religion.

Keirsey, D., and M. Bates. *Please Understand Me*. Del Mar, CA: Prometheus Nemesis Press, 1979. This book provides good character descriptions of the various combinations of psychological type profiles.

Kroeger, O., and J. Theusen. *Type Talk*. New York: Delacorte Press, 1988. This is a book geared for beginners that explains the concepts of type. In particular, the authors use some good examples to describe type differences.

Lawrence, C., A. Galloway, and G. Lawrence. *The Practice Centers Approach to Seatwork: A Handbook*. New York: McKenzie Press, 1988. This brief booklet describes how teachers can use learning centers to respect individual differences in their students.

Lawrence, G. *People Types and Tiger Stripes: A Practical Guide to Learning Styles*. Gainesville, FL: Center for the Applications of Psychological Type, 1979. This brief book describes how type concepts can be applied in education. The focus is primarily on the application of type at the high school and college level.

Meisgeier, C., and E. Murphy. *Murphy-Meisgeier Type Indicator for Children: Manual.* Palo Alto, CA: CPP, Inc., 1987. This is a manual for the *Murphy-Meisgeier Type Indicator for Children,* the type instrument that measures the concepts of psychological type in children in grades 2–8.

Meisgeier, C., E. Murphy, and C. Meisgeier. *A Teacher's Guide to Type: A New Perspective on Individual Differences in the Classroom.* Palo Alto, CA: CPP, Inc., 1989. This booklet introduces elementary and high school teachers to the concepts of psychological type and explains how it can be applied in the school setting.

Myers, I. *Gifts Differing.* Palo Alto, CA: Davies-Black Publishing, 1980, 1990. This book describes type theory. It also includes extensive examples. Because of its concentration on theory, it is not recommended as a first text for those new to type theory.

Neff, L. *One of a Kind.* Portland, OR: Multnomah Press, 1988. This book introduces type differences in children and provides examples of how an understanding of type differences can help families and schools better understand the differences of children.

Wickes, F. G. *The Inner World of Childhood.* Englewood Cliffs, NJ: Prentice-Hall, 1966. The text reviews aspects of child development and psychological type. A focus on theory is emphasized.

Index

About the Author

Elizabeth Murphy, Ed.D., is a licensed school psychologist who has worked with children from preschool through adolescence. She is the coauthor of the *Murphy-Meisgeier Type Indicator for Children* and frequently conducts training sessions on individual differences in children for parents and teachers. One of her goals is to teach adults and children about type as a tool for improving communication in the home and school setting. She has two children with preferences opposite on all four scales and a husband who shares only introversion with her.